W9-BMO-097

AFRICAN AMERICAN
ENTREPRENEURS
Stories of Success

By Philip Wolny

LUCENT
PRESS

Published in 2018 by
Lucent Press, an Imprint of Greenhaven Publishing, LLC
353 3rd Avenue
Suite 255
New York, NY 10010

Designer: Deanna Paternostro
Editor: Siyavush Saidian

Library of Congress Cataloging-in-Publication Data

Names: Wolny, Philip.
Title: African American entrepreneurs: stories of success / Phil Wolny.
Description: New York : Lucent Press, 2018. | Series: Lucent library of black history | Includes index.
Identifiers: ISBN 9781534560796 (library bound) | ISBN 9781534560802 (ebook)
Subjects: LCSH: African American businesspeople–Juvenile literature.
Classification: LCC HC102.5.A2 W65 2018 | DDC 338'.0089'96073–dc23

Printed in the United States of America

CPSIA compliance information: Batch #BS17KL: For further information contact Greenhaven Publishing LLC, New York, New York at 1-844-317-7404.

Please visit our website, www.greenhavenpublishing.com. For a free color catalog of all our high-quality books, call toll free 1-844-317-7404 or fax 1-844-317-7405.

CONTENTS

FOREWORD

Black men and women in the United States have become successful in every field, but they have faced incredible challenges while striving for that success. They have overcome racial barriers, violent prejudice, and hostility on every side, all while continuing to advance technology, literature, the arts, and much more.

From medicine and law to sports and literature, African Americans have come to excel in every industry. However, the story of African Americans has often been one of prejudice and persecution. More than 300 years ago, Africans were taken in chains from their home and enslaved to work for the earliest American settlers. They suffered for more than two centuries under the brutal oppression of their owners, until the outbreak of the American Civil War in 1861. After the dust settled four years later and thousands of Americans—both black and white—had died in combat, slavery in the United States had been legally abolished. By the turn of the 20th century, with the help of the 13th, 14th, and 15th Amendments to the U.S. Constitution, African American men had finally won significant battles for the basic rights of citizenship. Then, with the passage of the groundbreaking Civil Rights Act of 1964, many people of all races began to believe that America was finally ready to start moving toward a more equal future.

These triumphs of human equality were achieved with help from brave social activists such as Frederick Douglass, Martin Luther King Jr., and Maya Angelou. They all experienced racial prejudice in their lifetimes and fought by writing, speaking, and peacefully acting against it. By exposing the suffering of the black community, they brought the United States together to try and remedy centuries' worth of wrongdoing. Today, it is important to learn about the history of African Americans and their experiences in modern America in order to work toward healing the divide that still exists in the United States. This series aims to give readers a deeper appreciation for and understanding of a part of the American story that is often left untold.

Even before the legal emancipation of slaves, black culture was thriving despite many attempts to suppress it. From the 1600s to the 1800s, slaves

4

developed their own cultural perspective. From music, to language, to art, slaves began cultivating an identity that was completely unique. Soon after these slaves were granted citizenship and were integrated into American society, African American culture burst into the mainstream. New generations of authors, scholars, painters, and singers were born, and they spread an appreciation for black culture across America and the entire world. Studying the contributions of these talented individuals fosters a sense of optimism. Despite the cruel treatment and racist attitudes they faced, these men and women never gave up, changing the world with their determination and unique voice. Discovering the triumphs and tragedies of the oppressed allows readers to gain a clearer picture of American history and American cultural identity.

Here to help young readers with this discovery, this series offers a glimpse into the lives and accomplishments of some of the most important and influential African Americans across historical time periods. Titles examine primary source documents and quotes from contemporary thinkers and observers to provide a full and nuanced learning experience for readers. With thoroughly researched text, unique sidebars, and a carefully selected bibliography for further research, this series is an invaluable resource for young scholars. Moreover, it does not shy away from reconciling the brutality of the past with a sense of hopefulness for the future. This series provides critical tools for understanding more about how black history is a vital part of American history.

SETTING THE SCENE:

1619
The first slaves arrive at the Jamestown settlement in Virginia, beginning the era of American slavery.

1916
Brothers Noble and George Johnson start the Lincoln Motion Picture Company, the first company owned and controlled by black filmmakers.

1827
The first African American newspaper, the weekly *Freedom's Journal*, is established in New York by Reverend Peter Williams Jr.

| 1619 | 1810 | 1827 | 1861–1865 | 1893 | 1916 |

1810
The African Insurance Company begins operations in Philadelphia, Pennsylvania.

1861–1865
The American Civil War begins; Abraham Lincoln issues the Emancipation Proclamation; the Union emerges victorious from the Civil War.

1893
Charles Douglass, son of abolitionist Frederick Douglass, and his wife Laura Douglass establish the first black resort town in Highland Beach, Maryland.

A TIMELINE

2014
Dr. Dre, a musician and entrepreneur, sells his Beats headphones company to Apple for $3 billion.

2000–2004
BET founder Robert L. Johnson becomes America's first black billionaire; Oprah Winfrey becomes America's first black female billionaire.

1949
Jesse B. Blayton Sr. opens the first African American–owned and operated radio station in the United States: Georgia-based WERD-AM.

1949	1964	1991	2000–2004	2008	2014

2008
Barack Obama is elected as the first African American president of the United States.

1964
The Civil Rights Act outlaws discrimination on the basis of race, color, religion, gender, or national origin.

1991
Black Entertainment Television (BET) is the first African American–owned company to trade on the New York Stock Exchange.

INTRODUCTION
MAKING IT

In October 2009, two giants of American entertainment and media met for an interview: Shawn "JAY-Z" Carter appeared on Oprah Winfrey's television talk show. JAY-Z was a hip-hop legend raised in an underprivileged housing project in Brooklyn, New York, while Oprah was a Southerner from a tiny farming town.

Though they were of slightly different generations, they felt an almost automatic connection. One had grown up in the tough urban environment of the 1970s and 1980s in New York City. The other had experienced childhood through the late 1950s and 1960s, a time of great change in the South. Both had experienced struggle and had overcome many obstacles. These two moguls—despite their different paths and industries—had risen to the top of their fields from very modest means.

JAY-Z often includes details of his rags-to-riches rise from his poor childhood, including time spent as a drug dealer, in his musical lyrics. His course had taken him to lead several companies over a couple of decades' time, become the creative force behind a dozen solo musical albums, and emerge as a leading player in a number of other projects. Oprah survived terrible abuse during her childhood and teens in Kosciusko, Mississippi, before moving to Nashville, Tennessee, to live with her father. As an adult, she created an entertainment empire and rose to immense global fame.

A more important and obvious connection links these two famous success stories: Both are African American entrepreneurs. In the 2010s, many media personalities and academic voices have publicized the continuing double standards applied to white Americans versus non-whites in general, otherwise known as people of color, and African Americans in particular. The historical legacy has been especially painful for black Americans as they continue to search for and fight for equality in the United States. For many

JAY-Z and Oprah Winfrey, shown here, are among the most successful African American entrepreneurs in history.

black Americans, especially younger ones, success stories such as Oprah's and JAY-Z's serve as inspiration for their own dreams and hard work.

Overcoming Adversity

Much of American culture, from its very beginnings, has celebrated those who rise from poverty and obscurity to find great success. The drive, hard work, resources, and luck involved in opening even a small business are great. These factors are multiplied many times over for African Americans, many of whom have not only built businesses and corporations from the ground up, but have often done so while facing major racial discrimination.

The idea of the American Dream has been both a powerful inspiration and a sometimes frustrating myth for many throughout the history of the United States. Many cultural threads from many different groups of people have been woven into the fabric of this idea. The first European settlers of the northeastern colonies, also known as New England, were the Puritans, who settled and took the territories of modern-day Massachusetts from the indigenous Native Americans. They were well known for being strict with their religion and rules, but also for a very tough work ethic.

Despite many initial failures trying to work the unfamiliar land, it was partly this obsession with hard work that helped them survive and eventually thrive. This was accompanied by a sense of thrift and financial discipline, the ability to save money and resources for a future time, rather than spend too much and waste them in the present. The ability to live with less and make fewer resources stretch out longer was highly valued. Taken together, these values were identified by many Americans as the "Puritan work ethic," sometimes also known as the "Protestant work ethic."

As American agriculture, industry, power, and invention grew throughout the 19th century, this idea of a good work ethic became linked to the idea of the entrepreneur—that person with the drive and ambition to take chances and start their own business. Whether it was selling things people needed, providing services, or managing a store or restaurant, being an entrepreneur became a major part of the American Dream for many. This was especially true for both those with roots in the United States itself, including African Americans, and for the waves of immigrants from many different nations who flocked to the United States in the 1800s and after.

Rags to Riches

One author, in particular, became famous in the 19th century for his tales of young American teenagers rising from extreme poverty to achieve financial success. Horatio Alger Jr., born in 1832, did much to help create the concept and myth of the rags-to-riches story that has captivated Americans for centuries. His many young adult novels pushed what became known as the "Horatio Alger myth." In these books, a person, typically a boy from a humble background, achieves success through hard work and a combination of good fortune and skill to dig himself out from poverty and rise to the middle class or even reach great wealth. He generally succeeds with the help of a sympathetic, older, rich person who sees his true worth. The main character often accomplishes their ambitions by being brave or ethical in some impressive way, such as helping someone out on the street in a time of need, finding a large amount of money somewhere and returning it to its owner, or another display of good citizenship or morality.

"Yearning to Breathe Free"

For millions traveling to the United States from foreign lands to attain the American Dream, the message inscribed on the Statue of Liberty was a symbol of their journey and dreams. The imposing and famous monument in New York City's harbor was one of the first things new immigrants saw upon arriving in the United States, especially those who were processed through Ellis Island beginning in 1892. Inscribed at the base is an excerpt from an 1883 poem by Emma Lazarus, titled "The New Colossus." Lazarus wrote the poem to help raise money for the Statue's pedestal:

> *Give me your tired, your poor,*
> *Your huddled masses yearning*
> *to breathe free,*
> *The wretched refuse of your*
> *teeming shore.*
> *Send these, the homeless,*
> *tempest-tost to me,*
> *I lift my lamp beside the*
> *golden door!*[1]

Just as many native-born Americans with little or no wealth hope to one day rise to success, their immigrant counterparts hoped to do the same. However, with a 250-year history of slavery, stretching back to the beginnings of the colonies in the early 17th century, the black population has often been an abused and oppressed minority. Unlike immigrants who chose to give up their livelihoods and

This illustration shows slaves working during a cotton harvest on a southern plantation during the early 19th century.

past lives in their homelands, those who were shackled as slaves in colonial America until the final liberation of slaves in 1865 had little choice. They, too, have yearned to breathe free.

The descendants of slaves also had to face extreme hostility and hardship to even get on the same playing field as other Americans, if they could get there at all. There remains much work to do to achieve more equality, even into the 21st century. Despite progress, it seems that inequality has continued to exist, including the income inequality that has plagued black Americans since the time before the Civil Rights Era.

Perseverance: A Staple of Entrepreneurship

One of the qualities that many people consider part of the American experience is perseverance: the ability to stick with a project, goal, or dream despite extreme hardship and delay in achieving it. For entrepreneurs of any ethnicity or background, perseverance is an especially important quality. The ability to go on even when facing all kinds of obstacles makes someone strong in the face of problems that may overwhelm regular people and prevent them from reaching ambitious goals. It has been an especially vital quality for African American entrepreneurs to possess.

In addition to the normal stumbling blocks that anyone chasing their dreams experiences, black people have faced extremely high levels of poverty and inequality. Even after slavery officially ended, many black Americans were economically victimized, prevented from accessing full equality in property and business ownership, segregated by unfair laws, and provided inferior resources when it came to schools and other government services.

For the many decades of theoretically being free, African American communities have called out for social justice in the face of widespread abuses, especially when it comes to law enforcement policing their communities. Many African American parents not only give their children "the speech"—in which they warn them of their increased vulnerability to racism and police harassment—but also inform them how much harder they will have to work to prove themselves to their white peers.

Through it all, however, there have been many inspiring and successful black entrepreneurs dating back to the very beginning of U.S. history. These included both freedmen—those who had been granted or bought their freedom from slavery—and those born free citizens, in addition to immigrants from Africa and the Caribbean who arrived on their own to make their mark in the New World. African American entrepreneurs have excelled and experienced success in nearly every imaginable field and type of business. From banking and insurance to trade to publishing, music, film, and many other media, prominent African Americans have been part of the nation's entrepreneurial spirit from the beginning.

They have not only ridden the wave of business building and innovation that the United States has used to become a global superpower. Rather, African Americans have been at the forefront of business innovation in many fields. Later groups of black immigration have only added to this creative and dynamic culture. In turn, many African American entrepreneurs have taken their success and put money, resources, and their own hard work into improving their communities, especially when it comes to helping the workers and ambitious young entrepreneurs of the future. Whatever the shortcomings of the American Dream for many African Americans, many others have made it work for them. In the process, their stories serve as an inspiration to all Americans—not just African Americans. These are their stories of success.

CHAPTER ONE
BLACK ENTREPRENEURS IN EARLY AMERICA

Early America was a much different place than the country now recognized as the United States. It began with the original settlements by mostly European settlers, which eventually turned into the 13 colonies that banded together to fight and overthrow British rule. After that, the new nation of the United States expanded westward. The markets and economies of the growing ports and other towns and colonial territories were very important parts of everyday life, much as they are now.

Industry and mass production did not exist in the early days of America. Products were made mostly by hand by skilled craftspeople. Many of these crafters were part of the middle class. Banking and many other business enterprises were similar to today's methods, except they were done by hand on paper, and business activities happened more slowly than they occur in the digital age.

Slavery: America's Brutal Past

Many African Americans in early America had little involvement in the free markets of the time, at least not directly. Most Africans who came to the New World were brought against their will—as property. Many were not simply captured by the slave traders themselves but were sold by African, Arab, and European traders who had captured or bought them from others, including during military conflicts. The international trade in human beings was one of the earliest global business activities.

While their fates were often controlled by their owners and masters, it is a mistake to imagine enslaved Africans—and their children born into slavery—as completely helpless. Business, trade, and bartering, whether done secretly by slaves hiding from their masters or out in the

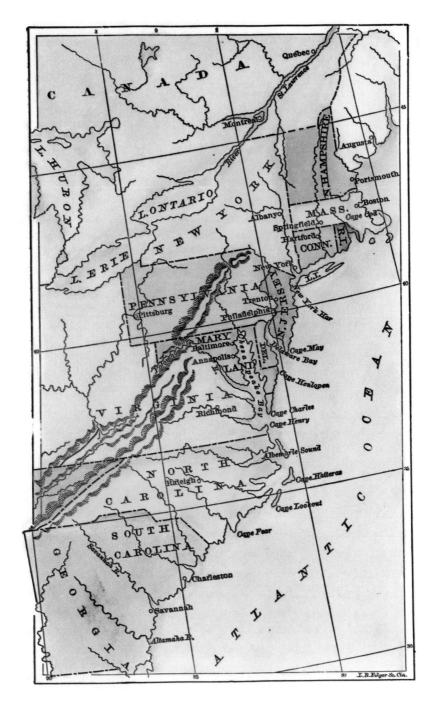

The original colonies along the East Coast of America joined together to form the United States in 1776.

open, were common activities. Even under the often terrible and hopeless conditions of slavery, there was an entrepreneurial spirit. Many people sold into slavery came from societies that had advanced business relationships and activities. According to one historian,

> *The West and West Central African victims of the transatlantic slave trade to the Americas came from complex, organized, and structured market economies in which they participated as producers, traders, brokers, merchants, and entrepreneurs ... They either produced market goods or were producer-traders, brokers, or merchants.*[2]

Still, the racist idea that Africans had been somehow "rescued" from a life of poverty and savagery in their home continent was a convenient lie that powerful whites spread. It helped justify slavery as a somehow moral and correct system; in reality, it was a horrifying and unjust one, and millions of Africans suffered because of it.

Black and Free in the Colonies

In some places, before slavery and the white government that ran it became overwhelmingly powerful, relations between blacks and whites were actually slightly more equal earlier in colonial times than they would later become. For example, in Virginia, it was possible for former slaves to become free and start businesses or become land and property owners with the right to vote locally. Free blacks even had relative equality and experienced greater justice in the court system than they would later have in the heart of the slavery era.

Slavery would grow to become the most profitable and important institution of the southern United States in the 19th century. In southern areas, it would erase or severely restrict the rights and privileges of any blacks. The institution existed nearly everywhere in the colonies until it was abolished in all northern states in 1804; New Jersey was the last northern state to outlaw it. In the North, there had never been as big a need for slave labor as in the agricultural states of the South. Slowly but surely, growing communities of free blacks began to pop up everywhere in America, largely in the North and even sometimes in the South. Many of them had earned their own money, even as slaves, and had bought their freedom from their owners.

Some free blacks had gained emancipation from their masters, while new

As this 19th century racially motivated painting shows, white people almost always viewed blacks as savages who were not equal to them.

laws freed others during the American Revolution, a conflict in which many blacks served on both sides. Many escaped bondage. Even more emigrated from the West Indies of the Caribbean. Thousands more free blacks became Americans when Thomas Jefferson (a slave owner himself) bought the territories of the Louisiana Purchase in 1803 from France's Napoléon Bonaparte. Bonaparte sold France's American territories to the United

Even in southern states during the 19th century, there were some free blacks, such as this group relaxing in Virginia.

States because his nation had lost so much money when the slaves of Haiti revolted against their French masters—a revolution the slaves won in 1804.

A Skilled and Diverse Workforce

Many black Americans had skills and experience with many kinds of work. In the North, freedom came earlier, and free black communities and populations had far greater opportunities. The greatest opportunities to start one's own business enterprise (outside of farming) lay in the cities, which, at the time, were not very large. The earliest and most important urban centers were the ports that helped America grow, including Boston, Massachusetts; Philadelphia, Pennsylvania; and New York City.

During the early 1700s, some African Americans in these cities owned property, made money from crafts and trades, and ran small shops, as well as catering businesses, barber shops, and other businesses. Most entrepreneurs made money with these small, service-oriented businesses. In some places, especially the South, laws would work against them in starting big agricultural businesses, participating in the slave trade itself, or dealing in large amounts of commodities; these were the jobs that produced great wealth.

In addition to being legally restricted, many of these lucrative opportunities worked via word-of-mouth social networks, and someone had to know an insider to get started. Racism was the largest contributing factor to these types of enterprises being generally closed off to blacks.

Finding Niches

Entrepreneurs always look for opportunities and often succeed where they find an opening for their services. This can mean finding a particular need that others have not satisfied yet or one that competitors have failed to provide; this is called filling a niche market. One niche market that was relatively new in the early 19th century was insurance for African Americans.

In Philadelphia, a city with a sizeable black community, several African Americans banded together to form the African Insurance Company in 1810. This was the first African American–owned insurance company in the United States. It grew out of one of Philadelphia's old beneficial societies, the Free African Society. Beneficial societies were groups of blacks who teamed up to support each other in tough times. Such groups charged monthly dues to create a pool of money to help their members when they got sick or passed away and required funds for funeral costs or to help their widows.

While the Free African Society was similar to what is today called a nonprofit organization, the African Insurance Company was formed to make a profit. Its founders—including Joseph Randolph (president), Cyrus Porter (treasurer), William Coleman (secretary), and Absalom Jones (director)—had seen an opportunity in the free African American community of

Absalom Jones was one of the earliest African American entrepreneurs, directing the African Insurance Company from 1810 until it closed in 1813.

their city, which had been growing quickly, and began with "a capital stock of $5,000,"[3] which they used to get their name spread throughout Philadelphia. While the company did not attract as many customers as it had hoped to and seems to have either downsized its operation or completely shut down by 1813, its example served as an inspiration for future firms, especially the many black-owned insurance companies that thrived after the outbreak of the American Civil War.

The early 19th century was also important because it was an era that saw free African Americans making real money. Moreover, they were also beginning to keep their possessions safe by using the same places as wealthy whites: banks and stocks. Banks, insurance funds, shipping companies, and other money-related corporations were often a favored investment opportunity for African Americans who were newly flush with income. In the South, one historian pointed out, new finance laws in the era of slavery may have excluded blacks, but they also gave intelligent African Americans opportunities slightly outside of the legal banking system that favored whites:

The most extensive banking activity of wealthy antebellum [pre–Civil War] blacks was in the informal sector, where they acted as [unofficial] private bankers. While holding savings for fellow blacks, they made loans with interest not only to blacks but also to whites, who did not want their precarious finances to be a matter of public record.[4]

A Gentleman and a Sailmaker: James Forten

One early entrepreneur from Philadelphia was James Forten, born a free man in 1766. Forten's life outside of business was just as interesting and colorful as his life in it. At the young age of 14, Forten served as an assistant in the Continental Army and was part of a crew captured by the British. Though he had just two years of formal schooling, he was an avid reader and was naturally curious and inventive.

In addition, before his death from an accidental drowning when Forten was a boy, his father had worked for a sailmaker named Robert Bridges. He had even hired his son to work alongside him in Bridges's factory. This experience had been one reason behind his war service, in fact. It was also what led him to work on a transatlantic ship and then in London shipyards after the American Revolution was over. In 1785, Forten apprenticed with Bridges again.

James Forten was an extraordinary businessman and community leader; he was one of the first highly successful black entrepreneurs in America.

Despite some of the deep-seated prejudice still prevalent around Philadelphia, Forten was later promoted to foreman because he was such a dedicated and capable worker. He rose to become a partner in the business and eventually bought it for himself after working there 13 years, overseeing an operation that employed dozens of people. He used his position as a successful businessman to fight for the black community in Philadelphia.

While historical details are not clear, Forten is also sometimes remembered for innovating a new type of sail and rigging. While some historians insist he came up with a brand new sail, other accounts claim it was a hand crank that hoisted sails much more easily then before. However, he was never issued an official patent for any invention, and many believe he simply took advantage of new sailmaking methods that were developing around the country at the time.

Forten eventually earned enough money to be considered a part of the upper class; he would be a multimillionaire by today's standards. His career was impressive for anybody of his era, and especially so because of his race. Rather than simply resting on his laurels, the sailmaking entrepreneur gave to political causes that he believed in, including black equality in the United States. It is estimated that he put as much as half of his fortune into the abolitionist cause, partly by supporting the newsletters and organizations of abolitionists such as William Lloyd Garrison, for whose *Liberator* periodical he contributed anonymous letters. He also helped found the Free African Society.

His work, both as a businessman and abolitionist, earned him the great respect of many, and thousands attended his funeral in March 1842. Forten was a shining example of the few self-made black success stories of the era. He also foreshadowed future African American entrepreneurs, who would achieve even greater success but still fought to protect and assist their black neighbors.

Thomas Day: Cabinetmaker and Craftsman

Another skilled African American craftsman who made a name and fortune for himself in the 19th century was Thomas Day. Wealthy planters in North Carolina were known for favoring classical architecture and finely crafted furniture to show their elite status. As such, there was a great demand for well made and beautiful cabinets. Much like many craftspeople of his time, Day had learned cabinetmaking from his father. He had also gone to school with white students during childhood, and he was literate and educated. He and his brother opened their own shop in Milton, North Carolina, in 1827.

Thomas Day developed a unique style of cabinetmaking, using fluid lines and spirals that distinguished his furniture designs from other cabinetmakers, and thus became especially popular among the rich consumers of his state. These included important politicians, government offices, and the University of North Carolina at Chapel Hill. Day was so well respected that in 1830, when he married Virginia native—and free black woman—Aquilla Wilson, the state government (including the state's attorney general) agreed to make a special exception for him. This was because North Carolina passed a law in 1826 prohibiting free blacks from moving into the state.

Day was even more unusual in that he owned stock in the State Bank of North Carolina and had substantial real estate interests, which even many white people in the region lacked. He reportedly even owned slaves, with historical documents declaring that he had six, including some who worked in his business. Perhaps the greatest contradiction was that he had white employees and apprentices who, technically, enjoyed a greater social position than their boss yet were managed—and paid—by him.

By the time of his death in 1861, Day had left behind a legacy not only of expert craftsmanship, but also of a unique approach and vision for design that applied to both furniture building and the construction of detailed and interesting living spaces.

Clara Brown Goes West

Blacks, in general, suffered some of the greatest discrimination and prejudice in American society dating back to its beginnings. However, things were often even worse for black women, who had an even lower social position for much of U.S. history than their male counterparts. While blacks would struggle for equal voting rights for nearly a century after the Civil War ended slavery in 1865, black men could at least vote according to federal law, while women were to be denied that right—among many others—for longer still.

Nonetheless, many women persevered and even made their fortunes in a society that actively fought against granting them full rights. Clara Brown was a powerful example. She was born a slave in Virginia in 1800, eventually moving with her owners to Kentucky. She worked the fields from childhood. As an adult, she experienced the terrible tragedy of being separated from her husband and four children at an auction. This was a common fate for many black families of the era.

At the age of 56, in 1856, Brown received her freedom and was immediately required, by law, to leave Kentucky, which was a slave state. She settled in St. Louis, Missouri, working for a local merchant at first. When his family relocated to Leavenworth, Kansas, Brown's boss helped her set up a laundry business there. Soon after, Brown decided to go westward, joining a stream of people heading that way to make their fortunes searching for gold, farming, and other opportunities. It is believed that Brown may have been the first African American woman to make it to the Colorado Pikes Peak Gold Rush that began in 1858. She was searching for opportunity, but also hoped to find lost family members, based on rumors and information she had previously tracked down.

Brown's subsequent successes are a testament not only to black women, but also to the older generation. She was nearly 60 when she began working in Central City, Colorado. She opened her own business, doing laundry for the huge rush of prospectors and miners who were on their way westward. She also dedicated a lot of her entrepreneurial energies to establishing cooking, cleaning, and catering businesses alongside her laundry. By the time the Civil War ended in 1865, she had saved up $10,000—a remarkable amount.

She wisely channeled her profits into mining investments that yielded massive returns. It only took her several years to become a major property and claim owner in the area, owning large portions of land in around Central City. She then reinvested her profits to establish a supportive and racially equal community.

Like many black entrepreneurs of the time, Brown was a pious Christian, and her faith and kindness guided her to contribute greatly to charity and to help many others personally in her community. She included not only African Americans, but also whites and Native Americans in need. She earned an affectionate title of respect, "Aunt Clara," for her willingness to take in and care for the sick and poor.

Her money also gave her the resources to try and track down her long-lost children. Though she had heard rumors that her husband and son had passed away, she tried to track down her daughter Eliza. Though unsuccessful at first, her search resulted in her bringing a number of her other relatives and acquaintances out of eastern states and to Colorado, helping them find work and shelter. A few years before her death at the age of 82, Brown

Clara Brown was not only an entrepreneur, but she was also among the first African Americans to find success in the Wild West.

FROM SEGREGATION, A MIDDLE CLASS

Even as many blacks remained enslaved in the South throughout the first half of the 19th century, with others struggling in poverty on both sides of the country, the black middle class emerged in some areas and grew steadily. Relations between blacks and whites varied from the colonial era through the early 19th century, but even in areas where slavery had been outlawed, the races were generally separated. This was true even in areas where blacks and whites worked, ate, and shopped in the same parts of town.

Middle-class whites generally avoided contact with middle-class blacks in professional settings. As such, white people would likely not hire black professionals as their lawyers or doctors or retain them for other services, such as undertaking funerals or cutting hair.

This discrimination had something of an upside, however. The black professional class had its own market that was pretty much guaranteed: other African Americans. Businesses thrived selling services, professional or otherwise, to members of their own community. Everyone needed medical care, legal assistance, haircuts, and other services while they were alive and to be prepared to be laid to rest when they passed away. As the black middle class gained economic power, its members teamed up to build businesses together, create professional associations, create and help charities, and fund their own schools and universities. In turn, they reinvested their profits in the black community, trying to bring everyone else up with them.

eventually located and visited her daughter. Brown became the first black person and first woman inducted into the Society of Colorado Pioneers.

Samuel T. Wilcox, Grocery Store Pioneer

Around the 1850s, Cincinnati, Ohio, was a boomtown. Business was thriving for those who took advantage of a big surge in population in what was then one of the largest American cities. Among these was a boat steward, later a businessman, named Samuel T. Wilcox. Wilcox opened a wholesale and retail grocery business in 1850. Over time, he became known as the largest seller of groceries in the city.

He was innovative in that his business also may have been among the first ever high-end grocery stores. It stocked products targeted especially at wealthier patrons, including fine hams and other meats, canned fruits, high-quality soaps, dried fruits, sugar, molasses, expensive liquors, and cigars. On the side, he ran a pickling and preserving operation.

Samuel T. Wilcox took advantage of Cincinnati's large market of newly wealthy settlers to grow his grocery business into a retail giant. Like many other African American entrepreneurs, he fought to achieve racial equality.

BOSTON: A BEACON OF BLACK BUSINESS

More than one-third of the black population of Boston, one of the most important cities of colonial America, was free by the middle of the 18th century. By the early 1780s, all black Bostonians were free. Much of Boston's black community was centered in the Beacon Hill neighborhood. Boston served as a success symbol for black entrepreneurs from as early as the colonial period.

One major successful market for black Bostonians was apparel and clothing. By 1830, there were dozens of African American–owned clothing shops, as well as dressmakers, seamstresses, and tailors. Like many tailors and others in the colonial apparel business, most operated out of their homes. In the 19th century, African Americans were among the leaders in high fashion tailoring in Boston. Around the midcentury, some earned as much as $10,000 a year, which was a remarkable amount of money.

Other sectors in which black businesspeople thrived included: investing in real estate; running rooming and boarding houses; the hair and beauty industry, in which they worked as barbers, hairdressers, and wigmakers for both black and white clients; catering and hospitality work; and professional sectors, such as law, medicine, education, and the clergy.

Wilcox established links with sellers in New Orleans and New York, and by the middle of the decade, his business was selling about $140,000 worth of goods annually. After achieving such great wealth, Wilcox had spearheaded many ventures. While his grocery business was his foremost operation, he also ran a hotel called Dumas House. Additionally, he was known as a co-organizer of an all-black real estate investment collective known as the Iron Chest.

The First Black Millionaire

The story of William Alexander Leidesdorff Jr. is a distinctly American one. It takes place against the backdrop of a nation growing by leaps and bounds, as America expanded west. Leidesdorff was born in the Virgin Islands—then a territory of Denmark—in 1810. His father was a Danish sugar planter, and his mother was a native woman of the islands, partly of African descent. As a young man, he sailed on

William Leidesdorff Jr. proved to be an influential early citizen of San Francisco, California, even before it became part of the United States.

trading vessels that moved between New York and New Orleans, eventually becoming a captain once he became a naturalized citizen of the United States.

In 1841, Leidesdorff bought the *Julia Anne*, a 106-ton (96 mt) trading ship he sailed from New York to Yerba Buena, which was then part of Mexico and would later be named San Francisco, California. It was there that he truly became successful. Leidesdorff operated the first steamboat to run in San Francisco Bay. He also opened the city's first hotel, the City Hotel, and the town's first commercial shipping warehouse. He purchased 35,000 acres (14,164 ha) of land around the current site of Sacramento after he became a naturalized Mexican citizen. There are few people in San Francisco's early history that had as much of an impact as he did.

His influence continued to grow as Mexico was on the verge of losing California and other western territories after the Mexican-American War ended with a victorious United States. Leidesdorff hosted both visiting American and Mexican officials at his home. According to the Museum of the City of San Francisco, "Whenever government officials, American or Mexican, came to town, Leidesdorff's home, the largest and most impressive in the area, was always chosen as the scene for lavish state entertainment. He had the urbanity of a seasoned diplomat, politician, and man of affairs."[5] He served in a number of political and appointed positions in San Francisco, including the first town council, the first school board overseeing the city's first public school, and its first city treasurer.

When he died of a brain ailment in 1848, Leidesdorff was a wealthy man. Combined with gold discovered as part of his property, his worth is estimated to have been around $1.5 million, making him America's first millionaire of African descent.

CHAPTER TWO
FREEDOM, STRUGGLE, AND PROFIT

The American Civil War, a rebellion by a collection of southern states that wanted to maintain the institution of slavery, was one of the darkest times for the United States. After hundreds of thousands of deaths on both sides and unparalleled destruction, the Union defeated the rebelling Confederate States of America. Abraham Lincoln's Emancipation Proclamation went into effect on January 1, 1863, declaring that all slaves held in the Confederacy were free, but it was only in April 1865 that most hostilities ended with the Union victory and that freedom could be enforced.

The early optimism and hope that African Americans would now receive justice and freedom produced mixed results in the coming years. The era of Reconstruction after the war meant that the states that had rebelled were admitted back into the Union. They were forced to draft new state constitutions in which slavery was outlawed and in which free blacks would enjoy equal rights. This would importantly include full voting rights. Other federal and state government efforts during Reconstruction aimed to provide employment and shelter for both freed slaves and for those generally displaced by the war, including white citizens.

Reconstruction initially helped African Americans a great deal. Hundreds of blacks were elected to state and local government offices, and many of them favored laws that helped white and black citizens alike. As time passed and the federal government ended its military enforcement of new laws in the South, many southern states began to reintroduce unfair laws against blacks. Thousands of former Confederate soldiers and supporters regained the right to vote, voting whites into office. Unfair arrangements, such as the tough rules

This painting of Abraham Lincoln shows him with a copy of the
Emancipation Proclamation being read to his cabinet members.

of sharecropping, prevented many blacks from getting ahead.

A host of new laws—referred to as Jim Crow laws—created systems in many southern states in which racial segregation was strictly enforced. From about 1877 to the middle of the 20th century, Jim Crow became a way of life in the South. Blacks were routinely terrorized and murdered, prevented from voting, and denied the same rights as their white neighbors. Dozens of branches of a secret, racist terrorist organization called the Ku Klux Klan were behind much of the violence directed at black communities.

Segregation and unfair practices against black renters, businesspeople, and common citizens were also widespread in the supposedly freer and progressive North. Still, even with so much stacked against them, African Americans forged on. As the nation grew, populations expanded westward to new territories. The Industrial Revolution also continued in the northeastern states. Soon, a new era of African American entrepreneurship took hold.

The Great Migration and the Golden Age of Black Business

Many scholars and historians recognize the era from the turn of the 20th century to about 1930 as a golden age of black business in America. Huge cultural, social, and legal barriers stood in the way of many blacks' progress, but nonetheless, many entered the middle class via hard work, ambition, and the support of other African Americans. This included beneficial associations, some of which had been founded decades earlier. Many others were newly organized. African American entrepreneurs and other middle-class blacks were the backbone of these groups. They had extra money, also known as disposable income. Others, however, were not so lucky.

Many who worked the land ended up renting land from other owners, typically whites. Often, the terms of the land contracts were very unfavorable to the renters. Depending on the state, area, and arrangement, the renter paid the landlord with a share of the crop, rather than money. The renter would also borrow or buy equipment, seed, and other essentials from the landlord on credit. These would be added to the rent owed at harvest time. The system as a whole was called sharecropping.

Sharecroppers often remained in debt to landlords for long periods. They could not move if they were in debt. Many historians, scholars, and sharecroppers considered the system only slightly better than slavery itself. The challenging existence of this kind of farming and the abuse many blacks suffered at the hands of whites under segregation in the Deep South made many want to leave. In addition, vast changes in American agriculture drove southern unemployment higher.

Millions moved north for new opportunities. What historians have named the Great Migration began around 1910 and really ramped up during World War I when the United States needed many more workers for industry in northern cities to contribute to the war effort. Similar spikes in migration happened during World War II in the 1940s and then continued for decades until about 1970. In those decades, approximately 6 million African Americans left the rural South to settle in the industrial North.

Though the North gave many African Americans much better opportunities than the South had, it was not a paradise. In many cases, discriminatory laws, bad living conditions, and other problems plagued them. Huge numbers had come into close contact with each other in new communities, though, and this created incredible business opportunities for intelligent and talented entrepreneurs.

Booker T. Washington and the National Negro Business League

One individual who was not exactly an entrepreneur but still an incredibly important African American figure was Booker T. Washington. He was also controversial, because he believed black advancement relied on gaining economic power and then wielding it, rather than by fighting for civil and political rights. Many black activists and leaders criticized Washington for this stance.

One of Washington's great accomplishments was leadership of the Tuskegee Normal and Industrial Institute (now Tuskegee University) in Tuskegee, Alabama. At age 25, Washington began running the school at the recommendation of his mentor, a former Union general who supported black self-improvement. The school was enormously successful under Washington, becoming a leading institute of higher education. It trained black students in dozens of trades and professions, and upon Washington's death in 1915, it had a modern, 100-building campus; a 200-member faculty; and a $2 million endowment.

Washington launched the National Negro Business League in 1900 to train and prepare African Americans

Booker T. Washington was one of the most influential African Americans of his time. He inspired countless young blacks to succeed.

for the realities of the economy and financial discipline. His hope was that blacks would prove to whites their abilities and demonstrate their equality as people. It was designed to help and encourage blacks to start their own businesses. Its members were both established professionals and business owners in addition to blacks who were part of the middle class or trying to join it by launching their own enterprises.

The League had chapters throughout many states and localities. Its meetings allowed different people to meet each other and network, or establish business and professional relationships. Members also shared stories about their successes or obstacles. The League also had many white benefactors who believed in Washington's mission. He and other League members, in turn, used the group to help blacks network with whites, as well. Washington even made an impression on powerful white captains of industry and finance, such as Andrew Carnegie, a steel tycoon and one of America's richest men.

Maggie Walker, Bank President

Born in Richmond, Virginia, in 1864, just as the Civil War was winding down, Maggie Lena Walker graduated school in 1883, having trained as a teacher. She did not remain an educator for long, putting it aside when she got married because of legal boundaries that did not allow married women to teach.

However, she had been active since her teenage years in an organization named the Independent Order of St. Luke. The Order had been set up to help members pay for funerals and burial costs for themselves and family members. It had grown to do different charitable works and provide different forms of help to its African American members. With more free time since she was not teaching, Walker dedicated herself to working for the organization.

By 1899, when she was 35, Walker had risen to the organization's top leadership position: grand secretary. One of her first efforts to improve and expand the Order was launching a newspaper, *The St. Luke Herald*, to keep members and others informed about the organization and other events important to the community, including promoting educational work. Not long after that, Walker chartered the St. Luke Penny Savings Bank. The bank itself would become a huge success. Because Walker was its leader, she became not only the first black woman to charter a bank

Maggie Walker was a groundbreaking entrepreneur, becoming highly successful despite racism and sexism.

THE "BLACK WALL STREET"

The name "Black Wall Street" has been applied to different American black neighborhoods and business districts. One was the Jackson Ward neighborhood of Richmond, Virginia. Yet another was Durham, North Carolina, which was famous for good relations among blacks and whites. It was also well known for black-owned financial services firms, such as banks and insurance companies.

The third Black Wall Street was perhaps the most famous—and infamous. This was Greenwood in Tulsa, Oklahoma. By 1921, nearly 10,000 black residents lived in Tulsa, and many had built thriving businesses. These local companies were helped and supported by the relatively large African American population. Black entrepreneurs got an even bigger boost when a local oil boom in the 1910s caused the population to dramatically increase.

However, Greenwood would fall victim to a racist mob's violence on May 31, 1921. Tensions flared when a young black man was accused of attacking a white woman in an elevator. White mobs then attacked black men and women for two days straight. They burned dozens of square blocks of homes and businesses, mostly in the Greenwood neighborhood. As many as 300 people were killed, and hundreds more were injured. Much of one of America's most lively and prosperous black business communities was obliterated. Greenwood's business community eventually rebuilt some of what was lost, but the traumatic wounds did not heal so easily. The riot of 1921 is widely considered one of the worst single episodes of racially motivated violence in American history.

in the United States, but also the first woman of any race to charter and serve as a bank president.

By 1924, the bank served 50,000 members spread across 1,500 local chapters. Even when the Great Depression wiped out many financial institutions in the 1930s, Walker kept the bank alive by merging it with two others in 1929. This larger financial institution became the Consolidated Bank and Trust Company, and the chairperson of its board of directors was none other than Walker herself. It would continue on for decades as a major black-owned bank in the Richmond, Virginia, community. Walker's ability to grow the bank was matched by her efforts to expand the Order itself. By the mid-1920s, it had 100,000 members in dozens of states. She understood that self-sufficiency and cooperation were key to helping black Americans advance. "Let us put our moneys together; let us use our moneys; let us put our money out at usury among ourselves, and reap the benefit ourselves,"[6] she once said.

Seemingly nothing could stop the energetic Walker. In addition to the bank, in 1905, she even opened a department store called the St. Luke Emporium, which was especially geared toward employing African American women and providing discounted goods to its members and the black community in general. Even a diagnosis of diabetes late in her life could not hold her down. Around 1915, the condition ended up paralyzing her legs, and she would spend her remaining days in a wheelchair. However, she continued to work. In the process, she inspired not only African Americans and women, but people with disabilities, too.

The Patterson Family Business

New inventions of the industrial age would help transform existing businesses. This is what happened to Charles Richard Patterson and his family. Born a slave in Virginia in 1833, Patterson later escaped and settled in Ohio. There, he worked as a blacksmith for a business that built horse-drawn carriages. Eventually, he went into business with J.P. Lowe, a carriage manufacturer. They built a successful business over the next two decades. In 1883, Patterson bought the whole business. He renamed it C.R. Patterson & Sons Carriage Company. It achieved a moderate level of success under his leadership.

When Charles Patterson died in 1910, it was a time of invention and innovation. His son, Frederick, inherited the company, but he knew the business needed to change with the times if it was going to survive. The era of actual horsepower was fading, and Frederick switched over to building and servicing automobiles. Their first car, the Patterson-Greenfield, sold for $850 and was comparable to the Ford Company's Model T. They made about 150 of them. It was the nation's first black-owned car company.

Rather than continue with the tough prospect of competing with the incredibly powerful Ford, Patterson wisely changed up his business. Patterson & Sons switched to making bodies for trucks and buses that Ford or General Motors would use. He also renamed the company the Greenfield Bus Body Company. He had realized that school districts in the region would start switching to school buses to move students

THE BLACK ENTERTAINMENT BUSINESS IN THE JAZZ AGE

In the 1920s, millions of Americans joined the new, rapidly growing consumer economy. Many people call it the Roaring Twenties, because the economy was booming, industry was expanding, and people had plenty of money to spend. It is also called the Jazz Age due to the exploding popularity of jazz music. Jazz was an innovative and exciting new musical form created and largely performed by African Americans in urban centers all over America.

Many black jazz entertainers made decent money during this era. Many African Americans—including musicians who took their performance profits and reinvested them—also became entrepreneurs in the growing entertainment industry. These included owners of legal and illegal bars (called speakeasies), concert halls and other performance venues, wedding and event halls, restaurants, hotels, and many other places where people could relax and enjoy themselves. Some also became record producers, owned recording studios, and manufactured and sold the records.

During the early 20th century, Jim Crow laws meant traveling African American musicians often used segregated accommodations and often played to segregated audiences. Black entrepreneurs took this bad situation and made profits off of it. The large collection of performance spaces nationwide that catered to black jazz, blues, soul, other artists became known as the chitlin circuit, named after a favorite soul food dish.

around. Thus, he found his niche. Over time, Frederick Patterson built strong relationships with these buyers. Still, the business, just like many others, suffered irreparable setbacks during the Great Depression. Frederick Patterson died in 1932, but his son Postell kept things running until the company was forced to shut down in 1939.

Annie Malone: Missouri Makeup Maven

Another woman who made her mark during the golden age of black business was Annie Malone. She was part of the emerging generation of African Americans who had been born after slavery had been abolished. Malone was born Annie Turnbo in Metropolis, Illinois, in 1869, and her parents were once slaves. They passed away when she was young, and she was raised by an older sister in Peoria, Illinois.

When Turnbo was entering womanhood, black women were abandoning old hairstyles. They were adopting a newer, more fashionable look that had long been popular among whites: straight hair. Many thought this change looked to the future, establishing a more equal footing with other races that had naturally straight hair.

Turnbo became interested in hair and different ways of changing and styling hair. She was intrigued with the challenge of finding methods to straighten black hair in new ways. This meant doing so in a way that did not damage the hair or scalp, which was a problem with many contemporary methods, including using lye, which is a strong and harsh chemical. She used knowledge from her high school chemistry classes to experiment with new techniques.

Not long after, Turnbo started to make her own hair care concoctions. By the time she moved to Lovejoy, Illinois, with her older siblings, she was ready for business. She created and manufactured her own black hair care line that would not damage hair and scalps. Naming her product the Great Wonderful Hair Grower, Turnbo took her new business to St. Louis, Missouri. She hired a few people and had them sell her product door-to-door, a common and popular way of marketing products at the time.

Positive reviews and user testimonials soon spread about Turnbo's line of hair products. Another fine marketing touch she employed was naming a particular hairstyling method of hers "The Poro Method." The name was derived from a West African language, and it symbolized physical, emotional, and spiritual growth. It gave buyers the idea of an African identity, or branding, to her line of products.

In 1902, she opened her first store in St. Louis. Turnbo also flooded local newspapers and magazines with advertisements selling her line and hosted press conferences to get her name out. By 1910, her business had to move to a larger space due to its success, and she spread to the national level. Her Poro agents sold her line everywhere, and she had to copyright her brand and products to prevent others from copying her and profiting from her ideas. She is regarded as one of the first black female millionaires.

Annie Turnbo became Annie Malone after her 1914 marriage to

This image shows a group of graduates from Poro College.

Aaron Malone, an educator and Bible salesman. In 1918, she truly made history when she opened Poro College. It was the first American educational institution that specialized in black cosmetology. Poro combined the cosmetics business with education, and it employed a large and capable staff, including faculty, salespeople, and more. They not only taught students how to do hair and makeup, but also how to present a professional workplace image.

Annie Malone earned great wealth from her products and school, and she also gave back tremendously. Much of her money went to worthy causes, especially in and around the St. Louis area. Malone raised most of the money for—and was board president of—the St. Louis Colored Orphan's Home. It later bore her name, as the Annie Malone Children and Family Service Center.

Harry Pace

Born in Covington, Georgia, Harry Pace was raised by his mother. He went on to graduate at the top of his class from Atlanta University. The historian and civil rights activist W.E.B. DuBois was one of his teachers there, and they even produced a magazine together for a short while. Upon graduating, Pace worked for a printer and later, in insurance and banking. It was when he moved to Memphis, Tennessee, in 1912, however, that he found his true calling. He teamed up with W.C. Handy, and they became a songwriting duo. They soon formed the Pace and Handy Music Company and relocated to New York City's Harlem neighborhood. There, they worked with both classical and big band jazz composers and musicians for a few years, but Handy and Pace soon parted ways.

Pace borrowed about $30,000 in 1921 to start his Pace Phonograph Corporation. To the public, the part of the company that signed musical artists was known as Black Swan Records—named after Elizabeth Taylor Greenfield, a 19th century singer nicknamed the Black Swan. The blues, jazz, and gospel singer Ethel Waters was Pace's first big signing. Her success helped Pace's company, which he started out of his own basement, go far in its first year.

By summer 1922, Pace had hundreds of agents and dealers selling his records worldwide, 30 employees in a new headquarters, and even an 8-person orchestra to play on recordings. He had turned his early investment into $100,000 of annual income.

Profits quickly trailed off, however. Pace had not struck deals with radio stations, which soon became the major platform when marketing records to the public, and Black Swan folded. Despite his short run of success, Pace's efforts opened the door for other African American entrepreneurs, who now saw how profitable records could be. Some of his artists also got publicity from their time with him, and they went on to good careers. Pace himself bounced back. He opened the Northeastern Life Insurance Company in Newark, New Jersey. It would later become one of the North's largest African American–owned firms. A year before his death in 1943, Pace, who had earned a law degree in 1933, even opened his own law firm in Chicago, Illinois.

The North Carolina Mutual Life Insurance Company

Among even the greatest African American businesspeople of all time, it is impossible to overstate the importance of Charles Clinton Spaulding. Spaulding, the son of wealthy farmers in Whiteville, North Carolina, got his first taste of work on his parents' land. Because the schools in his area were not very good, at age 20, he moved and joined his uncle, Aaron Moore, in Durham, North Carolina. Moore was the first black doctor to practice in Durham. At age 23, Spaulding graduated high school.

He became a grocery store manager but then became interested in a new industry just beginning to take hold among African Americans, both in Durham and nationwide: insurance. Spaulding became general manager of North Carolina Mutual and Provident Association in 1899, which was co-founded by his uncle and another well-known black entrepreneur, John Merrick. The company's main service was burial insurance.

Spaulding wasted little time in growing the company. He hired insurance agents, many of them ministers, teachers, and other middle-class blacks respected in the community. He stayed general manager until Moore passed away in 1923. He then became president of the company, a position he held until his death. Its name eventually changed to North Carolina Mutual Life Insurance Company.

The company had been Merrick's idea, initially, but Spaulding's leadership grew it from a modest income to one of the largest insurance companies in the country. Spaulding himself became very wealthy. In 1921, he had also taken over Mechanics and Farmers Bank, which had grown out of North Carolina Mutual. He also

Insurance entrepreneur Charles Clinton Spaulding made big waves in the white-dominated field of underwriting.

held leadership roles in other branches of the company and other Durham underwriting firms.

Spaulding was one of the major players that made the city of Durham such a center for African American commerce. Important figures of black business and culture would visit Durham and comment on how well the black population was doing; even the poorer African American residents seemed to enjoy a higher standard of living than many of their peers throughout the South.

Spaulding was also a philanthropist and supported many civic, educational, and social organizations and groups, such as the YMCA and Boy Scouts of America. These also included black colleges, such as Howard University, Shaw University, and North Carolina College. In the 1930s, he did a lot of work for the Urban League to help connect African Americans with resources provided by President Franklin Delano Roosevelt's New Deal recovery policies after the Great Depression did so much damage to the economy. By the time of his death in 1952, North Carolina Mutual was the largest black-owned business in America, with assets of more than $40 million. Today, the company has $14.1 billion in active insurance.

CHAPTER THREE

THE POSTWAR YEARS TO A NEW ERA OF BLACK BUSINESS

As the United States entered the middle of the 20th century, its citizens, white and black alike, had gone through a great deal. The Great Depression, which decimated the economy and left millions unemployed and homeless, was immediately followed by World War II. However, the United States had emerged from the war with a powerful military, political influence, and industrial power. It became the leader of the free world.

African Americans, however, had unequal access to the political and economic power and prosperity. Discrimination was still widespread, and the best jobs were mostly only open to whites. Nonetheless, most people were doing better than they ever had throughout the nation's history. The U.S. economy was also changing; new inventions, an advanced highway system, good factory jobs, and high disposable income for many people of all classes made the postwar era one of great opportunity. Television and the film industry had grown to join radio and print publishing as huge businesses. All sorts of new products and services were being advertised to the consumer mass market, which was growing tremendously year after year.

The midcentury was also a time when African Americans would step up for their civil rights while continuing to be pioneers of entrepreneurship. They would reach for economic power and independence on their own terms. Mass media, important musical movements created by African Americans, and other industries would soon have black success stories to call their own.

The Civil Rights Era and Self-Determination

The era of Jim Crow and segregation had remained in place for nearly a century following the end of slavery.

Black activists, with support from sympathetic whites and others, had never given up fighting for their rights. From the late 1950s until the mid-1970s, the United States was rocked by protests, riots, and activism against racial discrimination and inequality.

Even against this backdrop, black entrepreneurs continued to change nearly every industry and field they worked in. Musical genres with deep origins in black traditions, including rock and roll, soul, and doo-wop, became hugely popular in America and worldwide, with audiences of all backgrounds. Prominent African Americans in the arts, politics, culture, and academia also pushed for black political rights and self-determination. The largely peaceful civil rights movement and the more radical black power movement influenced the African American public and caused major shifts in businesses run by people of any race.

Berry Gordy, Founder of Motown Records

In postwar America, the car was king. Because of this, Detroit, Michigan, which was the center of the U.S. automobile manufacturing industry, was one of America's richest and most important cities. One native of the "Motor City," as Detroit was often

called, would put the city on the map for music, too. Berry Gordy was born in Detroit in 1929. His parents were supposedly tough on their eight children, and were both entrepreneurs themselves. At a young age, however, Gordy wanted to become a professional boxer. After winning a series of fights, he was drafted into the U.S. Army to serve in the Korean War in 1951.

His army savings helped fund his first business: a record store he opened upon his return in 1953 named Three-D Record Mart. It went under, but it seemed that all the time he spent listening to jazz and other music there had gotten under his skin. He knew that he had a talent for music, having won a talent contest with a song he had written in high school, so he began to think seriously about the music industry. While he worked other jobs, Gordy began writing songs. Soon, he started selling some to Decca Records, which recorded the songs with other singers. By 1959, he had quit everything else to write songs professionally. However, he realized the real money and success was in owning the actual songs.

With money earned by co-writing songs for his friend, soul singer Jackie Wilson, Gordy took the advice of another musician friend—the future soul

As a young man, Berry Gordy was unsure of where to take his life; he ended up becoming one of the most influential record executives of all time.

legend Smokey Robinson. His advice was to combine his savings with a small loan from Gordy's father and start his own record and production company. In 1959, Gordy merged several projects into one: the Motown Record Corporation. The name Motown referred to the Motor City, which was where his company was based.

Gordy tapped into several genres that, when mixed together, would take popular music by storm: black pop, rhythm and blues (R&B), and soul music. Soon, some of the most talented African American artists were flocking to his new studio, which was located in a building affectionately nicknamed Hitsville, USA. These artists included Smokey Robinson and the Miracles, the Marvelletes, Martha and the Vandellas, and other massive superstars. Gordy also had a natural instinct for picking the best songwriters, engineers, studio musicians, and production to support his artists. He carefully controlled the artists' images, making sure they were squeaky clean to appeal to the widest possible audiences.

Over the coming decade of the 1960s, some of the bestselling and most critically acclaimed African American musical artists of all time would record and sell records with Motown. These included Diana Ross and the Supremes, the Four Tops, the Commodores,

Stevie Wonder, and the Jackson 5, who featured arguably the most famous pop icon of all time: Michael Jackson. Motown was considered a hit factory. Many of Gordy's acts not only dominated the black charts, but they also crossed over by appealing to huge white pop audiences, too. There was rarely a week in the 1960s when there was not a Motown artist on the charts.

Gordy moved Motown to Los Angeles, California, in 1972, reportedly because he wanted to turn one of his most successful acts—Diana Ross—into a movie star. The company saw some successes in the 1970s by producing musicals, films, and television, but its days of unquestioned domination were behind it. Still, even in 1988, Motown properties were so beloved that a large entertainment corporation, MCA, bought Gordy's stake in the company for $61 million. For more than a decade, Gordy led his independent entertainment empire and changed the music industry forever—making quite a profit while doing so. His net worth in the 21st century is nearly $350 million.

John H. Johnson, Publishing Giant

Hailing from Arkansas City, Arkansas, John H. Johnson moved to Chicago as a teen in 1932. Born in the middle of the Great Depression, Johnson entered the

BLACK AND PROUD: THE 1960s

As civil rights activists secured victories for black voting rights and the beginning of the end for Jim Crow laws and their official, legal segregation, many black people began to take even greater pride in their identity. They witnessed these political successes and the great achievements of the black middle class—including those of entrepreneurs. This gave them pride in the fact that they could overcome hardships and stay strong against persistent racism.

One of the most popular artists among American audiences in the 1960s was soul singer James Brown. His 1968 hit, "Say it Loud—I'm Black and I'm Proud," with its chanted lines of racial empowerment sung by a children's chorus, perfectly symbolized this new feeling. There were many ways this message would be marketed to black customers. It also inspired many entrepreneurs to take chances, open businesses, and sell products of interest to their communities.

Black pride has often resurfaced with each new era of music since the civil rights movement. In the 2010s, Beyoncé Knowles made a powerful and famous statement of black pride and self-empowerment with her "Formation" song and video, which she performed at Super Bowl 50 in 2016.

world as it was going through a challenging time. His family, like millions of others, was forced to seek government help. It inspired him to work harder later on in life so he could be self-reliant. In an interview, Johnson once said, "I was a working child. I learned to work before I learned to play."[7] At an awards dinner for outstanding scholars, Johnson got to meet Harry Pace, the recording and insurance entrepreneur. Pace gave him a part-time job to help with schooling costs. While Johnson did not go on to finish college, the meeting and job stayed with him.

Similar to many success stories, he took his time finding the right path. With just a small amount of money saved in 1942, Johnson invested in a publishing business—Johnson Publishing—and started working on his first magazine, which he named *Negro Digest*. This was Johnson's black-focused version of *Reader's Digest*, the popular literary magazine. He had gotten the idea during his job working under Pace. He would later change its name to *Black World*. A magazine distributor took a liking to Johnson and helped him get the publication onto newsstands in Chicago and elsewhere. He was soon selling tens of thousands of copies every issue.

His more famous publication followed soon after, in 1945, and it was inspired by *LIFE* magazine, which printed news, general interest stories, and award-winning photography. Johnson called this monthly *Ebony*, and he filled it with articles about black public figures, news items of interest to the black community, and much more. *Ebony* quickly became the go-to source of news and light reading for millions of African Americans. He followed this extreme success with *Jet* magazine, which was a short weekly publication with an emphasis on news.

One of Johnson's main aims was to portray positive and empowering imagery of African Americans that would both attract sales and inspire his readership to achieve success. It succeeded beyond his wildest dreams, and its first print runs completely sold out all across America. The portrayal of blacks in its pages as regular, middle-class people also attracted all sorts of companies—and their advertising money—black and white alike.

Johnson also conducted smart market research. He convinced companies that ads with black people in them would do better among black consumers. Reflecting on the success of his publications, Johnson once said, "There were no major black models before *Ebony*, and there were few black salespeople for major companies before *Ebony*. I don't think we're completely responsible, but I don't know anyone who is more responsible."[8]

Johnson would become well-known beyond simply being a wildly successful publisher. *Ebony* and *Jet* also tapped into the spirit of the times. They reflected back to their black readers a positive self-image and a sense of racial pride. These publications also presented an image of African American success and dignity to the world.

Along with this vision of black pride, Johnson did not shy away from supporting the civil rights movement. In fact, he was a strong supporter of Martin Luther King Jr. and other important black leaders of the 1960s. More importantly, Johnson's writers and reporters covered the activists and their churches from the inside, rather than as distant observers. Their coverage really brought home the hope, heartache, and human impact of the civil rights struggle.

In 1972, the Magazine Publishers Association named Johnson Magazine Publisher of the Year. In 1982, he achieved another major milestone when he was included as one of the *Forbes* 400, which is a list

John H. Johnson is pictured here in his Chicago office with his daughter and copies of several of his influential publications.

of the most successful and wealthy people in the United States.

Baking Up a Business

In the latter half of the 20th century, chain businesses of all kinds exploded on the American landscape. Some of the most successful were restaurant and other food service chains. The model of McDonald's, in which entrepreneurs sell the brand, identity, and rights to start a restaurant to others, called franchisees, became one of the most common business models in the world.

One native of Tallahassee, Florida, lived an unusual life before becoming known for a nationally successful baked-goods chain. Wallace Amos Jr. lived with his aunt Della in New York City after his parents divorced. They lived humbly, with little money to spare, but were happy. One unforgettable sensation for him was the smell of the chocolate chip cookies his aunt regularly made. It was one of the things that inspired Amos to attend the Food Trades Vocational High School. His two years there gave him a solid background for a future in cooking—especially baking.

First, however, Amos would make a detour. After serving four years as a member of the U.S. Air Force, he came back to New York in 1957. He worked for a department store, and then he secured a job in the mailroom of the William Morris Agency. For decades, this company had been among the most famous and powerful agencies that managed Hollywood talent and other performers. Amos worked his way up the ladder of that company, slowly but surely. In 1962, he made history by becoming the firm's first African American talent agent. Through a mutual friend, he was able to sign Simon & Garfunkel, a famous folk-pop musical act. He led the rock and roll department for William Morris for a few years before leaving the company.

Ready for a change, Amos moved to Los Angeles in 1967, where he tried but failed to start his own management company. Even after watching his first business fail, Amos's entrepreneurial spirit could not be restrained; he quickly turned to his childhood love of baking, planning to open a cookie shop. Specifically, he was going to sell a modified version of his aunt Della's cookies that had brought him so much joy as a child. His many wealthy friends, made over the course of his time at William Morris, supported his idea enough to give him an initial infusion of cash. One of his early backers was Marvin Gaye, the R&B singing legend.

In March of 1975, the Famous Amos

Wallace "Famous" Amos, cookie entrepreneur, is shown here.

cookie shop opened its first store on Sunset Boulevard in Hollywood. The first year was good, but the second tripled his business's income, bringing in about $1 million in sales from three of the store's branches. One idea that Amos borrowed from a few other innovators was to also market his cookies in boxes to supermarkets. He began with the upscale New York department store Bloomingdale's. Soon, Famous Amos cookies were in grocery stores nationwide. Other companies began to emulate his success with this strategy.

The company only continued to grow for the next 10 years. However, things started to decline around 1985, and Amos's profits fell off. He sold off parts of the company to investors, and in 1988, he was forced to sell much of the remainder to the Shansby Group, an investment organization. Amos stayed on as a paid spokesman before quitting. His entrepreneurial spirit would resurface with new franchise ideas over the coming two decades, including the successful Uncle Wally's Family of Muffins, which were sold in stores nationwide. Amos also wrote motivational books about business, and he has been an advocate for literacy, helping thousands of youths and adults learn to read.

From Quiet Storm to Living Loud

Cathy Hughes grew up in a musical and motivated family in Omaha, Nebraska. Born Catherine Woods, her mother Helen Woods had been a trombonist. Her father had attended Creighton University, and he was the first African American to earn an accounting degree there.

During her 1950s childhood, Cathy daydreamed about broadcasting. In an interview with National Public Radio (NPR), she said, "I did my radio show every morning in the mirror with a toothbrush, and everyone thought at that time there was something wrong with me. I mean, there are no black people in radio, particularly no black women."[9]

She began her career in 1969 with an Omaha station, KOWH, and also worked at a local African American newspaper, the *Omaha Star*. In her position at KOWH, she was highly successful, spreading awareness and increasing listenership numbers for her employer. She left, however, to become a lecturer at the School of Communications at Howard University, a famous historically black college. Hughes's success was especially remarkable because in addition to her heavy workload, she was also raising a child as a single mother until she married Dewey Hughes.

She joined Howard's station, WHUR-FM, and by 1973, she had risen to be the station's general sales manager. Hughes increased station revenue more than 10 times over, to about

Cathy Hughes, one of the most successful African Americans in the history of radio, fought her way to the top of her field.

$3.5 million. One reason for this explosion in popularity was the emergence of a new radio format called quiet storm. This mix of soft pop, jazz fusion, and R&B ballads was elegant and easy on the ears. It had originated with a young show host at WHUR named Melvin Lindsey. With Hughes's support, quiet storm's popularity was an immediate success. Dozens of other broadcasters copied it, but it made WHUR one of Washington, D.C.'s most popular stations.

In 1978, Hughes joined a new station, WYCB. Despite her hard work, WYCB was still struggling to produce good numbers and profits. A meeting was called to figure out a solution, and the station's investors asked Hughes if she could help increase their profitability. She said she probably could, but wisely demanded an ownership stake in return. However, despite her proven success, the investors refused. She later told NPR, "One of the members said to me, if you think that you're smart enough to own a radio station, you should do it for yourself."[10]

She took this comment as a challenge. Hughes and her husband approached 31 banks for loans with a plan to buy a radio station, but they were turned down at every one. The 32nd bank, however, took a chance on her, and she secured the financing. It

was a risky, high-interest loan. Hughes also received help from Syndicated Communications, a group of wealthy investors who supported African American entrepreneurs, and bought WOL, a small, struggling radio station being investigated for corruption by the federal government, for $950,000 in 1980.

This was the beginning of the company she and her husband named Radio One. Despite early optimism, the station struggled for years. Hughes even lost her car and house, and she and her son lived at the radio station for a time. She told one reporter, however, that she "saw it as an opportunity to be there around the clock and learn how it operated."[11] The perseverance and hard work paid off. Slowly, after nearly a decade, WOL became profitable. Its parent company grew, too. Hughes drove much of the expansion when she switched the station to talk radio 24 hours a day. She hosted her own morning show for some time.

Soon after it began posting profits, Radio One started buying up other stations. By the late 1990s, it owned 70 radio stations spread among nine regional markets in the United States. In 1999, when Radio One was listed on the NASDAQ stock exchange, Hughes became the first African American woman to lead a publicly traded

INTEGRATION AND BLACK BUSINESS

The laws of the 1960s, though groundbreaking, did not cure racism, segregation, or other social ills facing African Americans at large. Most leaders believed much remained to be done. Millions of blacks were still in poverty, and racial tension continued to rear its ugly head. There were advances made in increasing the number of blacks entering the middle class, but there were also some unexpected side effects.

For one, the old successful black business districts in many cities began to decline or disappear. When segregation was the law, blacks could only really patronize businesses run by other African Americans. This made for a guaranteed, built-in market. With desegregation, African Americans spent more of their money all over town, including in white-owned businesses. This subtly changed the nature of black entrepreneurship. While thousands of black entrepreneurs start businesses every year, fewer of these are neighborhood staples that target African Americans. An area with a large black population may have a few black-owned hair salons and barbershops, some restaurants, and other services, but often, the businesses and the buildings that house them belong to a diverse group of owners and landlords.

corporation. She eventually brought in her son, Alfred Liggins, to help run the company, and as of 2016, they had a combined net worth of about $460 million.

Robert L. Johnson and BET

Television has been an extremely lucrative business ever since it first appeared in the middle of the 20th century. It was only natural that programming marketed and appealing to African Americans would be very profitable as well. As in most industries, there is a pioneer who sees an untapped market and takes advantage of it—and the undisputed innovator of black television is Robert L. Johnson. Johnson was born the ninth of ten children in Hickory, Mississippi, in 1946. Spending much of his childhood in Freeport, Illinois, he graduated from the University of Illinois in 1968 and earned a master's degree from Princeton University in 1972. He then moved to

BET founder Robert L. Johnson built his network into one of the most famous in America, and he used the profits to expand his business holdings.

Washington, D.C., to work in media and broadcasting policy.

He first worked for the Corporation for Public Broadcasting (CPB), a public nonprofit that helps fund hundreds of public television and radio stations and producers. Johnson also worked for the Urban League to help support African Americans all across the country. It was his work as a vice president of government relations for a lobbying group, the National Cable Television Association, that inspired his next business moves.

In 1976, cable television was becoming increasingly popular. Johnson saw that, aside from a few black sitcoms on network TV, there was very little programming directed toward African

American audiences. He called industry friends and ended up with a large pool of investment money in support of his idea to create a television network specifically catered to black viewers. In 1980, his vision was ready to launch, and the Black Entertainment Television (BET) cable channel became a reality. At first, it broadcast classic black films only a few hours a week on the East Coast. It did not even run on its own channel at first, but was hosted by Nickelodeon.

By 1983, Johnson had expanded BET into an all-day broadcasting giant that served U.S. and even Caribbean markets. It added reruns of classic black sitcoms, original programs, and music videos to its lineup. BET became immensely profitable by 1985. Its offerings then included sports, talk shows, stand-up comedy specials and comedy series, and news programming and political commentary. BET News, the first half-hour cable news program targeted specifically at African Americans, launched in 1988. The station continued broadcasting music videos, many of which BET broadcast first and then sold to MTV and other channels when they became popular.

BET broke barriers with more than just its content. In 1991, it was the first black-run business to be listed on the New York Stock Exchange. Tens of millions of households worldwide were loyal viewers. When Johnson decided to sell the network in 2001, it was bought by MTV owner Viacom for $3 billion. This sale made Johnson America's first black billionaire.

With this massive cash infusion, Johnson went on to found The RLJ Companies. This holding company is a large umbrella business that brings up different types of smaller companies. His investments include real estate and financial firms, hotels, casino gaming, and many other businesses. One of his most famous purchases was a majority stake in the Charlotte Bobcats (now the Hornets), making him the first African American to control a National Basketball Association (NBA) team.

CHAPTER FOUR

THE HIP-HOP GENERATION HITS THE BIG TIME

The 1980s and 1990s were times of great advancement for the black entrepreneurial spirit. More African Americans continued to move into the middle class, but at the same time, there were many left behind. Others became fabulously wealthy because of the new movements they created in the broadcasting, film, and music industries. In particular, one of the most important occurrences of the 1980s for African Americans, especially youth, was the growth of hip-hop culture and its main artistic medium: rap music.

It was the time of a new kind of businessperson, too. This type of entrepreneur had their first successes in one aspect of a business, and often branched out into many others. Many black entrepreneurs took their profits and then financed projects in completely different industries. A handful of black entrepreneurs had this Midas touch—it seemed that everything they put their hands on turned to gold.

Just as during segregation, but in a different way, the mainly white power structures and culture industries were little help to the new culture of hip-hop and the rap music industries. When powerful interests did come along, small-time hip-hop entrepreneurs feared losing a culture they had built up with their bare hands. Some responded to this possibility by becoming owners, producers, and distributors themselves.

The Robinsons

Sylvia Robinson was a veteran of the music business in the 1970s. The New York City native had started performing at age 14 as a professional musician under the name Little Sylvia. She was one-half of the duo Sylvia & Mickey, most famous for their chart-topping 1956 single "Love Is Strange." By the 1960s, she was married to Joseph Robinson and their family had relocated to New Jersey and set up their own label: All Platinum Records. Robinson herself sang on "Pillow Talk," an early disco hit produced by All Platinum, and the single eventually sold 2 million copies.

At the same time, a musical revolution was afoot in the streets of New York City's five boroughs. The Robinsons were in the right place at the right time to capitalize on it. Backed by Morris Levy of Roulette Records, the Robinsons formed a new label to put out an exciting new genre of rhythmic music called rap. Naming their new label after a famous district of Harlem, Sugar Hill Records was born.

Sylvia Robinson put together three young, inexperienced rappers from Englewood, New Jersey—Big Bank Hang, Master Gee, and Wonder Mike—and had them work on their rap lyrics and delivery, played over music sampled from a disco hit named "Good Times." The resulting group, the Sugarhill Gang, had a seemingly instant hit with the finished product, the massively successful "Rapper's Delight." It sold 8 million copies and put rap on the national map. The new musical genre, created by African Americans on the East Coast, would soon become known and loved worldwide.

Sugar Hill Records saw great success with the new rap scene. Other groups on the label were Grandmaster Flash and the Furious Five, the Treacherous Three, the West Street Mob, and the all-female rap group The Sequence, among others. The label also played a role in helping build the national rap landscape from the ground up and became part of a larger community of record labels, venues, and artists. It was truly a positive and exciting moment for a youth movement that arose out of a very tough time in New York's history.

Sugar Hill's Grandmaster Flash and the Furious Five would prove especially influential with their song "The Message," one of the first and most important politically and socially conscious rap hits. Altogether, under the Robinsons, the label had a huge impact on the future of a dynamic art form with great commercial potential. Joe Robinson made Sugar Hill the first label to put out cassette tape singles, helping replace the old vinyl format. Joe also also helped produce the Fresh Groove TV series, which played rap videos, including Sugar Hill's. The Robinsons saw the videos were the future of music marketing.

A botched deal with major label MCA and other pressures convinced

Sylvia Robinson, co-founder of Sugar Hill Records, was one of the early successes of the hip-hop movement

HIP-HOP: AN ENGINE OF ENTREPRENEURSHIP

From its beginnings, hip-hop culture embodied a can-do, do-it-yourself attitude. Its early artists, including DJs, MCs (rappers), b-boys (dancers), and graffiti artists, hailed from humble backgrounds. Few anticipated that they would make much money from the culture. Once the music became a hit on urban streets and spread all over the world, however, they were poised to profit from it.

Just like segregation ironically helped blacks develop their own middle class, the new, strange format of hip-hop made it seem unmarketable at first. There had even been a backlash in the late 1970s against dance-oriented music following the disco movement. Because of these reasons, major record companies avoided rap initially.

This created an opportunity for African American businesspeople to create their own companies on their own terms. Rap entrepreneurs cultivated networks of producers, record stores, and a performance circuit for their new music. They developed their own distribution networks and even developed their own clothing lines because major clothing brands were hesitant to sponsor rap artists at first.

Credibility and authenticity were important to hip-hop fans. This gave those within the culture—real African American artists—an advantage against outsiders who came in trying to exploit the new genre. Even when corporations realized the potential profits to be made from hip-hop, many of its street-level entrepreneurs had the leverage in recording negotiations, so they were given lucrative contracts.

the Robinsons to shut down Sugar Hill in 1985. Sylvia and Joe were divorced by this time, and Sylvia would only see modest success with future projects. However, for the great influence and inspiration she provided to a new generation of black artists, Sylvia Robinson earned yet another professional nickname: The Mother of Hip-Hop. Other labels that were founded around the same time Sugar Hill was failing—including Def Jam and others—would carry on the rap business and hip-hop culture.

Russell Simmons, a Founding Father of Hip-Hop

Russell Simmons, who became part of hip-hop royalty, came from quiet beginnings in the Jamaica neighborhood of Queens, New York City. Born in 1957 to city employees, Simmons graduated from high school and went to City College of New York in Harlem. His exposure to the Manhattan music scene through a fellow student brought him into the newly forming rap genre in the late 1970s, when he was in his 20s. His first taste of hip-hop culture was seeing an MC perform onstage in a small club.

Simmons found his niche business in the organizational and promotional aspects of the scene. He started promoting others, including rappers, and booking shows with them. He was not immediately successful, but he built a name for himself as a hard worker. In 1979, he had his first big break. A fellow student named Curtis Walker—rap stage name Kurtis Blow—worked with Simmons to produce a single named "Christmas Rappin," which Simmons promoted. It eventually sold more than 500,000 copies.

In the early 1980s, Russell's brother Joseph was a rapper with the stage name Run. Run went on to be one-third of the pioneering rap group Run-DMC, also from New York. It was Russell's idea to combine the group members' names to form the catchy Run-DMC. He helped them record a first single and get them on their way to becoming rap's first true superstars. The group would cross over from largely black audiences to appeal to fans all over the world. As the group grew bigger and more successful, Simmons helped manage the artists, as well as other rappers, including continued support of Kurtis Blow. They are regarded as some of the pioneers of the hip-hop movement.

Simmons's true success would be as a record label head. He teamed up with a New York University senior named Rick Rubin, who had become proficient in hip-hop production techniques. They found their first big artist together when they signed the charismatic young LL Cool J, also a Queens native. This was the beginning of Def Jam Records. Def Jam would truly take off with the runaway success of the first successful white rap group, the Beastie Boys. They would continue their winning streak by signing the legendary and innovative Long Island rap group Public Enemy. Def Jam made even more money when Simmons and Rubin signed a distribution deal with CBS Records.

Def Jam had greatly expanded by the late 1980s, including branching into several spinoff imprints. Simmons joined forces with music manager and promoter Lyor Cohen to form Rush Productions, later to be known Rush Artist Management. They also set up Rush Associated Labels to handle all of their musical output.

From the 1980s through the 1990s, Simmons seemed to have a hand in almost every imaginable famous and successful rap group in America. Rick Rubin, after disagreements with Cohen, would leave Def Jam to form a competing record label. Throughout the 1990s, various major labels would invest in or buy parts of Def Jam. Eventually, Universal Music Group bought the rest of the label from Simmons for about $100 million. Simmons had reportedly bought out Rubin's share for $120 million previously. Different spinoffs of Def Jam and its sub-companies would exist in some form until the mid-2010s.

Simmons was far from a one-hit wonder, however. The 1990s brought a new era for the diversified media mogul. This meant not only putting out music, but also investing in fashion lines, entertainment media, and also the newly emerging digital services online. Based largely on the influence of early entrepreneurs such as Simmons and his peers, hip-hop had grown from a grassroots music style made by underprivileged African American youth to an entertainment, fashion, and cultural movement worth billions of dollars.

Simmons had thought ahead and had put money into profitable businesses that reflected hip-hop culture and sensibilities. In 1994, he formed Rush Communications, which put out Def Comedy Jam, Def Poetry Jam, other broadcast specials, touring performances, and various other media ventures.

Other sources of income for Simmons have been his apparel companies: Phat Farm, American Classics Eyewear, and Argyleculture. Simmons has also funneled millions of dollars of his own money and raised money from others to support Rush Philanthropic Arts Foundation, which he formed with his siblings. The foundation helps underprivileged children—especially African Americans—access arts education and helps support emerging young artists.

With his many diverse ventures, Simmons has also served as a model for other moguls and entrepreneurs. Many successful individuals who built businesses in and around hip-hop culture, including Sean Combs, JAY-Z, Queen Latifah, and countless others, credit Simmons as a major inspiration.

Dr. Dre: West Side Success Story

The late 1980s and early 1990s would usher in an era of West Coast hip-hop. The Compton, California–based rap group N.W.A. took the scene by storm in 1988 with its hard beats and harder lyrics, popularizing a new, bold genre called gangsta rap. N.W.A. included future solo star and actor Ice Cube (O'Shea Jackson), and Eric "Eazy-E" Wright. Wright was also co-owner of N.W.A.'s label, Ruthless Records. The man responsible for bringing N.W.A. together and creating some of their most memorable songs was André Romelle Young, more commonly known as Dr. Dre.

Though Dre and N.W.A. did not invent gangsta rap, their music took the genre to new heights. Many cultural academics and African American historians consider the emergence of gangsta rap a revolutionary musical movement. Being an intelligent young businessman, Dre found a way to take advantage of the gangsta movement to create a profit. There had been socially conscious rap similar to N.W.A. before, but rarely had it been as openly confrontational and aggressive. The music's extreme profanity, along with gangsta rap's violent and often sexually explicit lyrics, was both appealing to many fans and dangerous to its rising popularity. Many major labels simply were not ready to sign such controversial acts. Dre, among others, marketed his music as fighting against the standards of American society. Millions of fans responded positively.

However, even other genres that the music industry found dangerous, such as heavy metal, did not spark as strong a backlash as hardcore rap did in the 1980s. Millions of parents across the country, angry that their children were listening to offensive music, demanded that the government regulate the music industry. The result of this was that the powerful Recording Industry Association of America (RIAA) began issuing stickers on records that read "Parental Advisory: Explicit Content." Rap fans often criticized such actions. They believed that there was a double standard applied to young artists of color that other musicians often were not held to. Still, even with barely any radio play or coverage on most television stations that played music videos, N.W.A. sold huge numbers of records.

When N.W.A. broke up, it was Dr. Dre who went on to be the biggest success. The rapper, producer, and entrepreneur co-founded Death Row Records with Marion "Suge" Knight, a former football player and club bouncer who reportedly had gang connections. Dre's first solo record,

The Chronic, would become one of Death Row's earliest smash hits. Knight and Dre would also profit handsomely from the music of Snoop Dogg, who became a superstar in the hip-hop community. They would see perhaps their greatest success by putting out the work of Tupac Shakur, one of rap's most beloved—and mourned—figures. He was murdered in 1996.

Dr. Dre would eventually leave Death Row to found Aftermath Entertainment, which would achieve massive sales from signing the rapper Eminem. One of Dre's smartest moves was launching his company to sell headphones, Beats Electronics, in 2008. His signature headphones were wildly successful, and in 2014, "Apple finally announced it has acquired headphone maker Beats Electronic[s] for $3 billion, including $2.6 billion cash up front and approximately $400 million in stock."[12] After this massive deal, Dr. Dre officially became one of hiphop's richest entrepreneurs, with a net worth of around $730 million in 2017.

Sean "Diddy" Combs: Hip-Hop Mogul

A native of Harlem, Sean "Diddy" Combs came of age just as hiphop began to truly explode in the mid-1980s. He made it to the prestigious Howard University before dropping out after two years. The aspects of college life that truly gripped him were throwing parties and events; like Russell Simmons, he found a passion for promoting. His experience in promoting parties and other hands-on work convinced him that four years was too long to wait to begin working toward his ambitions. He had booked some big acts to play at Howard and was hooked on the thrill of being at the center of it all.

Combs had grown up in the birthplace of hip-hop culture and absorbed the sounds of rap music during its underground golden age. He was inspired by Andre Harrell, the head of Uptown Records, which had been enormously successful with R&B, rap, and soul acts in the late 1980s. Combs aimed to be an entertainment executive, perhaps even heading a record label.

Combs turned to his friend, rapper Heavy D, who worked at Uptown under Harrell. In 1990, he was hired to work at Uptown as an intern. Combs soon greatly impressed the older mogul and everyone else at the company. He worked hard enough to get a major position at Uptown: vice president. He focused his energies on promoting and discovering new young artists. One of Combs's first hits was the up-and-coming urban boy band, Jodeci. He

Combs knew from an early age that he wanted to work in record production, and his entrepreneurial spirit helped him achieve his dreams.

made them popular by dressing them in the latest street fashions, which appealed to their fanbase. He also gave their music a makeover, adding harder hip-hop beats to their smooth R&B. Their debut album, *Forever My Lady*, sold more than 3 million copies.

Combs's next discoveries would catapult him and two more artists to superstardom and success. One was singer Mary J. Blige, who had been a talented musician for some time but had not seen much success. Combs saw that Blige's unique style and sound—combining hip-hop, R&B, and gospel soul—was an unbeatable formula, especially with her incredible voice. With his guidance, she went on to become a major star. Her solo debut, *What's the 411?*, went triple platinum and was a critical smash hit.

Despite these early successes, Combs was not getting along well with other members of Uptown's staff. In 1993, he was fired from the record company. Unwilling to let his dreams die, he started his own label: Bad Boy Entertainment. Around this same time, he cultivated a friendship with another talented newcomer to the hip-hop scene that would cement his success. Combs launched the career of Christopher Wallace, a Brooklyn native also known as the Notorious B.I.G. or Biggie Smalls. Before he was murdered in 1997, Biggie was one of rap's most influential and respected artists. His career seemed to have no limit. When he first signed with Combs, however, Bad Boy Entertainment was still a long way from being able to distribute Biggie's music effectively.

Combs soon found a new benefactor in Arista Records, a major label that agreed to a $15 million deal to distribute Comb's new Bad Boy musicians. Following a series of minor hits from some smaller hip-hop artists, Biggie's first album was released in 1994. The debut album, *Ready to Die*, truly exemplified the rapper, the producer, and the label's golden touch. The hugely successful album took both Wallace and Combs to the top of the music industry.

The rest of the 1990s would be a time of great triumphs—and tragedies—for Combs. Notorious B.I.G. was shot dead in March 1997 under mysterious circumstances, an event that was emotionally draining for Combs. Meanwhile, Bad Boy had become just one part of Combs's impressive business empire. Like Russell Simmons, Combs founded his own clothing company, called Sean John, in 1998. He also provided management to artists from other labels and signed profitable promotional deals with other brands and companies, including those with makers of luxury goods. In the 2010s, he is estimated to be the wealthiest hip-hop entrepreneur in the world, with a net worth of more than $800 million.

Magic Johnson: From Basketball to Businessman

Earvin "Magic" Johnson Jr. earned his basketball fame and his nickname as a young man while he was playing high school basketball. Spectators and reporters were so impressed with his accurate and intricate ball handling that they described his skills as magic. The nickname—and talent—stuck with him up through his time playing in the NBA.

Johnson became a famous star during a time when successful athletes were no longer just regional celebrities, but had joined to the ranks of multimillionaire superstars in entertainment, music, or other fields. Along with his peers, including the Chicago Bulls' Michael Jordan, Johnson earned tens of millions of dollars from playing basketball during his 13 seasons with the Los Angeles Lakers. He retired suddenly in 1991 (though he would come back for several exhibition games) because he discovered he had tested positive for the human immunodeficiency virus (HIV).

Unlike many sports stars of the previous generation, he used his money to transform himself from athlete to entrepreneur. Just as the 1980s moguls of rap and other musical movements diversified their businesses, Johnson would think outside the box to let his already huge fortune make more money for him. He started his company, Magic Johnson Enterprises (MJE) in 1987, knowing his time as a basketball star was winding down. Johnson also hoped to accomplish two things at once: become an entrepreneur and help create economic opportunity for African American youths desperate for work.

Among his first business interests were investments in underserved areas of his adopted hometown of Los Angeles, including: Magic Johnson Theatres, which expanded to several other cities; a number of Burger King franchises across the United States; and a chain of health and exercise clubs. Johnson also had a hand in T.G.I. Friday's and Sodexo, a French-based food conglomerate, and he opened Starbucks franchises to add to his investment portfolio. Johnson teamed with Canyon Capital to form the Canyon-Johnson Urban Fund, which has helped develop dozens of real estate projects all around America.

Johnson launched a cable television network in 2012 called

ENTREPRENEURS AND PHILANTHROPY

Many African American entrepreneurs donate to charity. Those who give discreetly, because they do not want to publicize their generosity, often do it through a religious institution, whether it is a Christian church or another faith-based organization.

Others make a point of being public with their giving to serve as role models, inspire others to give, draw media attention to the struggles of some kind of victim or disenfranchised group, or promote awareness about a medical condition or social justice issue. Some of the most prominent African American entrepreneurs are also prolific philanthropists.

Eddie C. Brown, founder of Brown Capital Management, one of the nation's oldest black investment management firms, has mainly given to promote achievement in public schools.

Russell Simmons, the rap and lifestyle mogul, has largely supported arts programs for youth and animal rights efforts.

Tom Joyner, a nationally syndicated talk radio and television host, set up the Tom Joyner Foundation to fund scholarships specifically for students attending historically black colleges and universities.

Hugely successful rapper, producer, and actor Ludacris started the Ludacris Foundation, which funds different groups helping homeless, abused, or neglected children.

ASPiRE TV, which is geared toward African American audiences, with an emphasis on positive and faith-based content. He formed Magic Johnson Bridgescape Academies to help at-risk students complete their high-school diplomas. Johnson has also worked tirelessly to combat the stigma associated with HIV, and he has given money to help develop treatments for those living with the virus. This included forming Clear Health Alliance, which focuses on HIV-positive patients.

During an awards show honoring him, *Sports Illustrated* magazine issued a statement praising Johnson, who they said spent "[A] life dedicated to creating opportunity for others as well as himself. Few athletes have done more with the stardom they gained between the lines of competition."[13] Johnson told *Sports Illustrated*, "I get asked if I'm trying to help minorities or make money. My answer is, 'I'm trying to do both.'"[14]

Queen Latifah: Musician, Actress, Producer

Few female stars of hip-hop have had as much success as Dana Owens, known to most of the world by her hip-hop and acting stage name, Queen Latifah. A native of Newark, New Jersey, she was first given the nickname "Latifah" in childhood, because it was Arabic for "delicate," or "sensitive." She attached Queen ahead of it as a stage flourish, the way many rappers would preface their names with Lord, Grandmaster, or King.

She benefited from the name once she began her rap career because it fit well with the Afrocentric trend of the late 1980s and early 1990s, which was an updated form the black pride movement that had been sparked during the 1960s and 1970s. In high school, her first group was named Ladies First, and she soon joined a crew named Flavor Unit.

She was only 18 when her demo landed in the lap of *Yo! MTV Raps*, a popular program that showcased music from the hip-hop movement.

Soon, the Queen was signed to a deal with Tommy Boy Records and released *All Hail the Queen* in 1989. She distinguished herself with her rapping talents along with her female-positive, feminist, pro-black, and Afrocentric lyrics. In styling herself this way through music, she influenced a generation of young female artists who came after her in the 1990s and 2000s, including recording artists such as Lil Kim, Foxy Brown, Lauryn Hill, Missy Elliott, Eve, TLC, and later artists, such as Nicki Minaj.

As the years have passed, Queen Latifah has been a model, talk show host, and, most notably, a well known, critically acclaimed, and award winning actress. She has acted in major feature films, including *Chicago*, *Bringing Down the House*, *Barbershop 2*, *Beauty Shop*, and *The Secret Life of Bees*.

Like many talented veterans of the hip-hop scene who have proved their ability to achieve long-term success, Latifah realized that ownership and being at the head of the production process offered the most profit and creative freedom. She co-founded Flavor Unit Entertainment, named after her old rap group, with partner Shakim Compere in 1995. Flavor Unit Entertainment, which also managed

Queen Latifah moved from her successful career as a rapper to a series of acting roles that took her to even greater fame.

musical acts early on, has gone on to produce many television and film properties. Some notable productions have been the film *Beauty Shop*, two different versions of *The Queen Latifah Show*, the VH1 series *Single Ladies*, and the HBO TV film *Bessie*, a biographic movie about blues legend Bessie Smith, with Latifah in the starring role.

CHAPTER FIVE

BREAKING BARRIERS AND LOOKING TO THE FUTURE

Though a number of unquestionable improvements have been made to the lives of African Americans in the 21st century, they still face equally unquestionable difficulties. The election of Barack Obama to the presidency in 2008 was an incredibly symbolic milestone for a nation with a troubled racial history. The thoughtful, intelligent new president and his first lady, Michelle Obama, have inspired countless African Americans of all ages with their examples of leadership, success, and family values.

Still, monumental problems face African Americans, other people of color, and marginalized communities in general. Inequality and mass incarceration prevent millions of African Americans, especially young men from impoverished areas, from reaching their full potential. Many of the public school systems that poor blacks attend are underfunded and inadequately staffed by teachers who give up on students before they even have a chance. As a result, becoming a successful black entrepreneur is still tremendously difficult.

It is no wonder that tales of African American businesspeople defying the odds and carving success out of sometimes awful poverty still inspire many to overcome those odds. Just as it has been since the founding of the United States, the African American entrepreneurs who make it big almost always give back and contribute to the communities they came from.

Oprah Winfrey, America's Most Successful Broadcaster

One of the most successful, influential, and admired people in the world is also one of the most accomplished and beloved African American entrepreneurs in history. Most people who have

TINA WELLS: ADVICE FOR ENTREPRENEURS

Tina Wells has been an entrepreneur for more than half her life. What is amazing is that she actually started her most successful business at age 16, in 1996. Buzz Marketing, based outside of Philadelphia, has been a groundbreaking marketing company that connects client businesses with the profitable, sometimes difficult to reach, and fickle youth market. Wells was targeting millennial consumers—people born in the late 1980s or 1990s—before their generation even had a name.

She gave *Inc.* magazine a few pointers on success, directed at aspiring entrepreneurs. Among these were:

1. There are no little people.

One of my biggest pet peeves is when people ignore my assistant or employees ... Today's assistant is tomorrow's vice president. How you treat people matters.

2. You can always make more money, but you can never make more time. Use your time wisely.

I'm more likely to be upset by a 30-minute delay in a meeting than a 10 percent reduction to an invoice! I always tell my team we can make more money, but we can never make more time. Focus on ways to be more efficient.

3. If you fail to plan, you plan to fail.

This doesn't mean that you need to script every detail of your life, but you need to have a roadmap. Even though I use the word "plan," I really mean you need to have a vision *... Can you see what it takes to get to that vision?*[1]

1. Tina Wells, "Best Advice I Ever Got: Tina Wells," *Inc.*, December 21, 2012. www.inc.com/young-entrepreneur-council/best-advice-i-ever-got-tina-wells.html.

Oprah is shown here in a television promotional still from her time spent as a local news anchor.

an Internet connection, television, or radio, or have even glanced at a magazine or newspaper since the 1990s, have heard of Oprah Winfrey.

Besides her incredible accomplishments, wealth, fame, and sense for business, one thing many people connect with is her background. Hers is truly a tale of persevering over emotional hardship, racial discrimination, and countless obstacles—and coming out on top.

Oprah Winfrey was born in rural Kosciusko, Mississippi, in 1954, a period that was still in the middle of the Jim Crow era. She spent her first years with her grandmother, in such poverty that she barely had wearable clothes. At age 6, she relocated to Milwaukee, Wisconsin, so she could live with her mother. She has told the widely publicized story that after she moved to Milwaukee, she was abused by several male relatives and people who knew her mother. In her early teenage years, she moved again, this time to live with her father in Nashville, Tennessee.

Winfrey was an avid reader, charismatic friend, and intelligent student. She did well in high school but was aware of the stark differences between her and many of the wealthier students in the suburban high school she attended. A speechmaking contest she won helped get her a scholarship to Tennessee State University (TSU). At TSU, a historically black institution, she continued with a job she had secured her senior year of high school: reporting news for a local station—her first real job in broadcasting.

Breaking Barriers

This job was merely the first of a series of stepping stones the talented Winfrey would take, as well as the first of many barriers she would shatter. She worked both in radio and television in Nashville and soon became the first African American female news anchor at WTVF in that city—and the youngest. In the 21st century, black anchors on television are much more common, but the mid-1970s were only a few years removed from the controversial and divisive civil rights era.

Winfrey continued to move up after her college graduation, this time joining an ABC station in Baltimore, Maryland, as a co-anchor on the evening news program. She would find her true calling, however, with the talk-show format after a new local talk show, *People Are Talking*, hired her as co-host. Her next step was to host her own show, moving in 1984 to an even bigger market: Chicago. Winfrey took over the morning talk show *AM Chicago* on a station there; the show had been struggling for a few years with bad ratings and low profits.

Her natural talent for talking with people—her guests, audience members, and the broadcast audience—was immediately apparent. The show exploded in popularity. Winfrey's ratings soon beat the powerhouse talk show in the Chicago market, *The Phil Donahue Show*. In 1985, just one year after taking command of the program, it was renamed *The Oprah Winfrey Show*. Taking the advice of her friend, movie critic Roger Ebert, Winfrey fought for a syndication deal, which meant broadcasting her show nationwide and generating even greater profits.

Her deal succeeded, and her ratings instantly shot to the top of the national list. Beyond mere ratings, audiences responded positively to the sensitive and confessional nature of Winfrey's talk format. To many viewers, she felt like the close friend they could confide in or the sister, aunt, or relative with all the answers in a time of need. Her show would become among the most popular and beloved TV shows of all time for its 25 seasons, ending in May 2011.

Her immense television success gave Winfrey tremendous influence and the financial resources to use it. She would expand her operation into one of America's most recognizable

and powerful media empires. She started a company to house all her different new businesses, using her name spelled backward, to launch Harpo Productions in 1986. She was the first woman to own a talk show after she bought her own program from her producers in 1988, including the studios where she filmed the show, and was one of the first women to own a large production facility.

Under Winfrey, Harpo produced programming such as *The Women of Brewster Place*, a 1989 television miniseries, her own talk show, and movie productions, the most famous of which were adaptations of important literary works by African Americans, such as Toni Morrison's *Beloved* and Zora Neale Hurston's *Their Eyes Were Watching God*. Winfrey was even an actress herself, having a major debut in 1985's *The Color Purple*, which is one of the most influential African American films of all time. She went on to have roles—some major, some minor—in some of Harpo's most successful productions.

In 1996, Winfrey launched a book segment on her show, called Oprah's Book Club, in which she and authors, critics, or celebrities discussed some of her favorite new works. Oprah would recommend that her viewers read and talk about her Book Club selections for the coming month. Due to her massive audience reach, inclusion in the Book Club often meant incredible sales for many authors, some of them previously obscure. This phenomenon of a book rising to global attention and shooting to the top of best-seller lists even had a name: the Oprah Effect.

Beginning in 2000, Winfrey produced *O, the Oprah Magazine*, and she maintains a popular website, which complements many of her other media properties and has millions of unique monthly users and 7 million members. She launched her own television network in 2011 called the Oprah Winfrey Network (OWN), which is available in 85 million homes. She had already co-founded the Oxygen Network with others years earlier. Her production company has put out shows by other popular talk show personalities, including Dr. Phil and Rachael Ray.

Winfrey's media empire made her a millionaire by age 32. In 2004, Oprah Winfrey achieved the incredible milestone of becoming the first female African American billionaire and is now reportedly worth about $3 billion. By 2006, she was the highest-paid television star in the United States, with a $260 million annual income. While she has slowed down her media empire in the 2010s, she remains one of the most influential women in the world.

Her charitable foundations and efforts—including the Oprah Winfrey Foundation, to which she has donated millions of her own money, and Oprah's Angel Network—have made Winfrey arguably one of the most generous philanthropists of the modern era and the most prolific African American donor of all time. She has financed the Oprah Winfrey Leadership Academy in South Africa, giving tens of millions of dollars toward supporting leadership among African women.

Besides financial success, Winfrey has inspired millions of African Americans, especially young girls, to succeed and dream big. She has also proven to be a role model to women of all backgrounds and to anyone who has struggled and overcome trauma to achieve their ambitions. There are few individuals who have so powerfully shaped how people—especially women—read, shop, exercise, and engage with the world. Many African Americans who follow trends in black culture and progress also praise Oprah especially for showing a positive and middle-class vision of black success.

Despite the poverty she initially rose out of, the racial discrimination she faced, and the abuse she suffered, her life's hardships did not slow down the queen of broadcasting. As she once famously said, "I don't think of myself

Oprah Winfrey's Leadership Academy—one of the most successful international women's empowerment organizations in the world—is just a part of her generous philanthropic efforts.

as a poor deprived ghetto girl who made good. I think of myself as somebody who, from an early age, knew I was responsible for myself, and I had to make good."[15]

Fashion Icon and Powerhouse Producer

The fashion industry means big business, and though models are the most visible representatives of fashion, a lot of the real powerhouses work behind the scenes. Tyra Banks has achieved success on both sides. Like many models, she entered the industry at a young age. Even with her appealing appearance, she still faced her share of discrimination and rejection due to her race. Despite prejudice, Banks became the first African American woman to appear on both *GQ* and *Sports Illustrated* magazines and spent years working for Victoria's Secret and other fashion designers. Eventually, she became one of the highest-earning models of the 1990s and 2000s.

However, the talented and motivated Banks would take a few pages out of the success playbook of broadcasting pioneer Oprah Winfrey to make her own empire off the runway. She began acting in films and television, but her main triumph came when she realized how popular reality television was becoming and decided to become a part of it. Banks launched her own production company, which allowed her the creative control she wanted—plus the financial returns. She named it after herself: Bankable Productions.

In 2003, Bankable launched the reality TV contest series *America's Next Top Model*, which ran on several networks, and reruns of it were still frequently broadcast despite the show's conclusion in 2015. The show later returned in 2016. Banks created the show as a competition to find a new top model every season, who the show would then reward with money and new modeling opportunities. Banks and the show both have been praised for their openness in fielding contestants of all backgrounds, including African Americans, other racial minorities, and those from the LGBT+ community.

They have also pushed to expand the acceptable standards of beauty in modeling, encouraging plus-size models to compete as well. It is an issue that Banks herself had to deal with, when critics made fun of her for being as much as 30 pounds (13.6 kg) heavier than the average model of her time. She proved her doubters foolish by going on to achieve massive success after switching from high-fashion modeling to swimsuit and lingerie modeling.

Few media stars have done what

Tyra Banks emerged from the modeling world as a high-powered business executive with a powerful entrepreneurial spirit.

A NEW, DIGITAL FRONTIER

With the rise of social media and the ever-increasing use of digital media, more young people are choosing to sell a wholly different product via video-sharing platforms such as YouTube: themselves. YouTube and similar websites allow users to monetize (or profit from) the videos they make, which encourages entrepreneurs skilled with technology to upload digital media. Some of YouTube's top young African American stars are listed below:

LaToyaForever entertains more than 1 million subscribers with personal anecdotes, funny stories about her family, and rants about things that annoy her.

Daym Drops has cultivated a fanbase of more than 700,000 subscribers who tune in to watch him review various types of food and restaurants. His videos have combined views of more than 120 million.

Kat Blaque is a transgender feminist vlogger who produces intellectual, critical videos about a wide range of social issues for more than 100,000 subscribers.

sWooZie is a professional gamer and animator. His 5 million subscribers make his humorous videos among the most popular on the site.

MyLifeAsEva, with her music, beauty, and comedy videos, is widely seen one of the site's rising stars, with more than 7 million subscribers.

Banks has done: host two popular television shows simultaneously. Debuting in 2005, *The Tyra Banks Show* ran through 2010 and won her a Daytime Emmy Award. Banks has widely embraced the modern standard of entrepreneurship: developing many revenue streams. In 2011, Banks launched an online destination dedicated to fashion and beauty. She also started Tyra Beauty, a cosmetics company, in 2014. To prepare for it, Banks even took classes at Harvard Business School.

From Studio to Runway and Beyond

African Americans have only rarely been as visible and successful in media and entertainment as they have been since the rise of popular rap in the 21st century. However, even with the success of some black models, including Tyra Banks, they have still been underrepresented as power players in fashion. One superstar who seemingly lives in the public eye is attempting attempting to change that: rapper-producer turned fashion mogul Kanye West.

Like Oprah in the early 2000s, there is almost never a week when West's name is not somewhere in the news. Often, it is for an outrageous or provocative statement or stunt, but few can deny that West is talented at keeping his name in everyone's conversations. He has also shown an aptitude for defying expectations and for following his own inspiration and vision, even if others might not immediately latch on to it.

West's earlier talents and successes were in the recording studio. He produced hit records and songs for JAY-Z's Roc-a-Fella Records in the early 2000s. Then, be became one of the most popular and prolific solo artists in recent memory, known for innovating and changing musical styles with each release.

Despite his huge success as a musician, West wanted to explore new territory to innovate in by starting his own fashion line. West knew he would face challenges, especially in being taken seriously. There are few major African American entrepreneurs in high fashion, much less ones who come out of hip-hop culture. West hoped to surpass the barriers broken by innovators such as Russell Simmons and Sean Combs, whose clothing was mainly targeted at black customers. West believed he could think bigger, broader, and better.

West approached the veteran athletic and casual apparel company Adidas as a partner. They were willing to take a chance and collaborate with him. West is beloved among his mostly young fanbase, making them a huge built-in market for anything he might put out. He also had bits of experience earlier working in fashion, including co-designing shoes with Nike, a shoe with A Bathing Ape, a streetwear brand, and other single projects.

Unlike many moguls who have started apparel companies, West was far more hands-on. He approached designs, colors, and every item in his collection the way a demanding producer tries to nail every beat, sample, or bit of instrumentation in a song. He took the unusual step of actually becoming an intern for major retailers and designers, such as Gap, Marc Jacobs, Fendi, and Raf Simons. West read one book of design after the next. He said about his mission to find his own voice and sensibility: "I have

Kanye West is shown posing here with models lined up in his Yeezy creations at New York Fashion Week in 2015.

that opportunity to put my name on something and people will buy it, but I want to create something that has its own voice and other designers can look to and be inspired. I wasn't put on this earth to make money—I was put on this earth to make magic."[16]

West has had several minor debuts at fashion weeks around the world, with mixed reviews. When his line with Adidas finally came out in 2015—dubbed Yeezy—it drew some of the biggest headlines of the fashion season. Still, some journalists and designers were angry about some of the publicity events surrounding his launches, saying that they took away from media coverage of other, less famous designers. Regardless, West continues as an underdog to try and do—in a completely new medium—what he has done in music: prove himself a self-made entrepreneur.

The Empire State of Mind

New York native Shawn Carter truly embodies the rags to riches narrative that people often identify with entrepreneurs. One of the most prominent African American entertainers of this millennium, the rapper, producer, and media mogul known as JAY-Z started with next to nothing. He grew up in the Marcy Projects, a low-income housing development in Brooklyn. For many disadvantaged African American youths in his circumstances, their chances of becoming both crime victims and criminals are far higher than their shot at becoming CEOs. JAY-Z has risen from the former to become the latter, however, smashing all obstacles in his way. Luckily, he had the talent as a rap artist to leave a teenage stint of drug-dealing behind. JAY-Z told *Vanity Fair*, "At some point, you have to have an exit strategy, because your window is very small; you're going to get locked up or you're going to die."[17]

When he hit adulthood, musical success came slowly but steadily. Then, he started producing hits in a huge wave. In addition to his solo albums becoming instant hip-hop classics and staples—including his 1994 debut, *Reasonable Doubt*—JAY-Z had the drive to make sure that his successes would profit him and not just others with the rights to his songs. He started Roc-A-Fella Records with partner Dame Dash and Kareem "Biggs" Burke. They eventually sold the company to Island Def Jam while still securing JAY-Z roles as company president and CEO in 2004.

Roc-A-Fella did not simply produce hit records. In 1999, JAY-Z and Dash also started Rocawear, their apparel company marketed toward urban youths, which also expanded to sell

JAY-Z is among the most successful black entrepreneurs of all time. His story—rising up from poverty to be worth millions—is a symbol of the American Dream.

JAY-Z is shown here at a 2010 breakfast meeting with Mayor Michael Bloomberg discussing the Barclays Center real estate development in Brooklyn.

kids clothing later, as well as accessories and luxury products. At its height in 2007, Rocawear was generating hundreds of millions in sales. JAY-Z later sold rights to the brand to Iconix Brand Group, retaining control over his personal share of the company, from which he still profits.

JAY-Z also started Roc Nation, an entertainment company, completely his own in 2008. One key aspect of the company was it was a full-service businesss: It housed a talent management agency, a record label, and production companies for touring and concert promotion. It also had branches dedicated to film and television production. One major aspect of its business was a multi-year, $150 million deal with LiveNation, which controls Ticketmaster and other live event entertainment businesses. It was renewed in 2017 for an additional $200 million.

Overall, the number of contracts and deals JAY-Z has signed and profited from over his career have been dizzying. The intelligent and talented businessman has risen from his low-income, high-risk background to command a digital and live entertainment empire worth more than $800 million. He is also married to pop singer Beyoncé Knowles-Carter, and the power couple is worth more than $1 billion combined.

The Next Generation of Entrepreneurs

A new generation of entrepreneurs is always on the rise, awaiting their shot at success. If they are successful, they rise to the occasion and become accomplished businesspeople. New opportunities are always arising for African Americans to be their own bosses. This is true for businesses that have always existed, such as restaurants and law firms, as well as new industries, such as digital marketing. The tools of the new, online economy open up enormous opportunities for those who may have little more than a good idea and an Internet connection.

In the 21st century, the obstacles for African Americans to begin new ventures might seem more troublesome than they have been in a long time. Many households—of all races—lost wealth during the recession that began in 2008. Plenty of entrepreneurs can afford to take chances with their families and communities behind them, but losing these resources—or lacking them to begin with—can derail any dream. However, the dreams and hard work of those fortunate enough to have support and those achieving success on their own have been and will always be the backbone of African American stories of business success.

NOTES

Introduction: Making It

1. Emma Lazarus, "The New Colossus—full text," National Park Service, accessed December 28, 2016. www.nps.gov/stli/learn/historyculture/colossus.htm.

Chapter One: Black Entrepreneurs in Early America

2. Juliet E. K. Walker, *The History of Black Business in America: Capitalism, Race, Entrepreneurship*, vol. 1. Chapel Hill, NC: University of North Carolina Press, p. 1.
3. Quoted in Walker, *The History of Black Business in America*, p. 112.
4. Quoted in Walker, *The History of Black Business in America*, p. 113.
5. Sue Bailey Thurman, "William Alexander Liedesdorff," Virtual Museum of the City of San Francisco, accessed January 2, 2017. www.sfmuseum.net/bio/leidesdorff.html.

Chapter Two: Freedom, Struggle, and Profit

6. "The St. Luke Penny Savings Bank," National Park Service, accessed January 2, 2017. www.nps.gov/mawa/the-st-luke-penny-savings-bank.htm.

Chapter Three: The Postwar Years to a New Era of Black Business

7. "John H. Johnson: The Voice of Black America," *Entrepreneur*, October 10, 2008. www.entrepreneur.com/article/197650.
8. "John H. Johnson: The Voice of Black America."
9. "'How I Built This': Cathy Hughes On Radio One," NPR, September 27, 2016. www.npr.org/2016/09/27/495595080/how-i-built-this-radio-one.
10. "'How I Built This.'"
11. William Reed, "Cathy Hughes: Black Business Icon," *Washington Informer*, November 3, 2016. washingtoninformer.com/cathy-hughes-black-business-icon/.

Chapter Four: The Hip-Hop Generation Hits the Big Time

12. Brian Solomon, "It's Official: Apple Adds Dr. Dre With $3 Billion Beats Deal," *Forbes*, May 28, 2014. www.forbes.com/sites/briansolomon/2014/05/28/apple-brings-dr-dre-on-board-with-official-3-billion-beatsdeal/#72b680a816d2.

13. Quoted in Ben Golliver, "Magic Johnson Recognized with Sportsman of the Year Legacy Award," *Sports Illustrated*, December 4, 2014. www.si.com/nba/2014/12/04/magic-johnson-sports-illustrated-sportsman-of-year-legacy-award.

14. Benjamin Snyder, "Magic Johnson: The Businessman Behind the Basketball Legend." *Entrepreneur*, December 9, 2014. www.entrepreneur.com/article/240734.

Chapter Five: Breaking Barriers and Looking to the Future

15. Peter Economy, "19 Empowering Quotes from Oprah Winfrey," *Inc.*, March 20, 2015. www.inc.com/peter-economy/oprah-winfrey-19-inspiring-power-quotes-for-success.html.

16. Quoted in Mark Beaumont, *Kanye West: God & Monster*. London, UK: Omnibus Press, 2015. PDF e-book.

17. "Jay Z on His Rags-to-Riches Story, Wooing Beyoncé, and How Blue Ivy Is His 'Biggest Fan,'" *Vanity Fair*, October 1, 2013. www.vanityfair.com/culture/2013/10/jay-z-beyonce-blue-ivy-story.

FOR MORE INFORMATION

Books

Bolden, Tonya. *Pathfinders: The Journeys of 16 Extraordinary Black Souls*. New York, NY: Abrams Books for Young Readers, 2017.
This detailed compilation gives summaries and information about some of black America's most respected figures.

Bundles, A'Lelia Perry. *Madam C.J. Walker: Beauty Entrepreneur*. New York, NY: Chelsea House, 2014.
This informative book, written by one of Madam C. J. Walker's descendants, details the amazing life of one of the most successful early African American entrepreneurs.

Charnas, Dan. *The Big Payback: The History of the Business of Hip-Hop*. New York, NY: New American Library, 2011.
This book traces the beginnings of entrepreneurship and business in the hip-hop movement through to the late 2000s.

Dingle, Derek T. *Black Enterprise Lessons from the Top: Success Strategies from America's Leading Black CEOs*. Hoboken, NJ: Wiley & Sons, 2002.
Various African American business leaders provide advice on how to excel in this comprehensive volume.

Winfrey, Oprah. *What I Know For Sure*. New York, NY: Macmillan, 2000.
A collection of newspaper columns written by Oprah Winfrey, this book provides the mogul's thoughts on a wide variety of issues and topics.

Websites

Black Enterprise (www.blackenterprise.com)
Black Enterprise is a monthly American magazine providing resources for African Americans interested in starting businesses and building wealth.

The Buy Black Movement (buyblackmovement.com/ Home)
The Buy Black Movement helps connect consumers with businesses to help promote black-owned businesses across the nation.

Center for Black Business History, Entrepreneurship, and Technology (www.laits.utexas.edu/ centerblackbusiness)
Hosted by the University of Texas at Austin, this website is an academic database with detailed articles about dozens of successful African Americans.

Entrepreneur Magazine (www.entrepreneur.com)
This is the website of *Entrepreneur* magazine, which carries frequently updated content on entrepreneurship, including featured articles about black businesspeople.

"25 Black Women Entrepreneurs" (www.essence.com/ galleries/25-black-women- entrepreneurs)
This article details some of the most successful female African Americans to ever open a business.

INDEX

PICTURE CREDITS

ABOUT THE AUTHOR

Philip Wolny is a writer and editor from Queens, New York City. He is the son of Polish-born entrepreneurs whose monthly magazine was once featured in the *New York Times*. He has written various young-adult titles, including *Money-Making Opportunities for Teens Who Are Handy*, *Getting a Job in the Construction Industry,* and *Getting a Job in Building Maintenance*. He has also written biographies about rappers and entertainers such as Ludacris and Sean "Diddy" Combs, as well as authors such as Stephen Chbosky and James Dashner. He lives with his wife Amanda and daughter Lucy in New York.